CAPTAIN of the QUEEN'S FLIGHT

Len Rush

with
Joy Chamberlain

BLOOMSBURY

First published 1987
Copyright © 1987 by Len Rush

Bloomsbury Publishing Ltd, 2 Soho Square, London W1V 5DE

British Library Cataloguing in Publication Data

Rush, Len
Captain of the Queen's flight.
1. Rush, Len   2. England—Biography
I. Title   II. Chamberlain, Joy
942.082′092′4   CT788.R84/

ISBN 0–7475–0013–4

Printed in Great Britain by
St Edmundsbury Press,
Bury St Edmunds, Suffolk

Early in 1962 Len Rush received a letter from the Queen's agent at Sandringham asking if he would go for an interview. Thinking that it might be the offer of some carpentry work, Len was astonished to learn that Her Majesty knew of his reputation as a pigeon fancier and wished to appoint him as her Royal Lofts manager.

Overnight the lofts at the end of Len's garden in a quiet street of King's Lynn were made ready for the arrival of the royal birds. Len chose just thirty-six from the excellent stock as the first generation of the Queen's flight he was to create. As soon as they were settled, the Queen came to Len's semi to see them and she returned nearly every year until his retirement.

For Len it was the high point of a life that began in a green Norfolk landscape, where as a child he was busy pig-keeping, crow-scaring and riding the giant horses that did the work of tractors on the farm where both his parents worked. That world has vanished now, long since bulldozed into a suburb of King's Lynn, yet through the richness of Len's recollections it exists once more. He brings to this memoir all the canny enthusiasm that made him so successful at his favourite occupation.

Len's delight in racing pigeons is shared by no fewer than a quarter of a million British fanciers. Competition is fierce but tempered by the profound respect all flyers have for their birds, and Len's story captures the quiet but thrilling spirit of the game. There must be a certain harmony in a loft that compels a bird to return to it at winning speed. Living today just 200 yards from the spot where he was born, Len Rush has realised such harmony himself and here delightfully invites us to come homing with him.

TO THE MEMORY OF MY WIFE, GLADYS, AND MY MOTHER

CONTENTS

ILLUSTRATIONS

PICTURE CREDITS

The author and publishers are grateful to the following for permission to reproduce black and white photographs: *Daily Star* (photo by Tim Cornall), no. 10; *Eastern Daily Press,* half-title, nos 8, 11, 16, 17, 18, 22; Keystone Press Agency Ltd (photo by Ian Tyas), no. 9; *Lynn News & Advertiser,* no. 12.

I

By Royal Invitation

My old mate Ernest Steele was manager of the Royal Lofts before me. He lived on the estate at Sandringham, in some converted stables, and for thirty bob a week he'd do some gardening there as well, at the agent's house.

He looked after the Royal Lofts for twenty-odd years and then he became ill, around 1959. I remember once he came off his bike in the snow, and he'd just lain there for ages, nearly freezing to death, because he didn't have the strength to get up again. For nearly four years the Queen's pigeons didn't race, and try as he might Steele could not keep the lofts ship-shape. An old-age pensioner would go there to clean them and feed the birds, but there was no one to train them. I would cycle from my home in King's Lynn to Sandringham every week, as I had done since before the War, to visit Steele and carry him news of the pigeon-racing world, which he sorely missed. Steele said not a word to me, but one day Major William Fellowes, the agent at Sandringham at that time, came to his house to ask him what they were going to do: the pigeons had to be set racing again. Steele could not have agreed more.

'I know just the boy for you,' he told Major Fellowes.

I wasn't a boy by anyone's standards other than Steele's, but he was Norfolk, like myself, and that's the way we speak.

Just after Christmas I received a letter from Major Fellowes, marked 'Strictly Private and Confidential', asking me to go to

Sandringham to see him. I thought perhaps there was some work for me there in the building line since by trade I'm a carpenter. 'As regards to conveyance,' the letter went on, I could go in my own car or one would be sent for me.

I rang Major Fellowes and said he wasn't to trouble himself, I would come on my bike. I've never learned to drive a car, let alone owned one.

'You can't do that,' said Major Fellowes.

'I can't come on my bike?'

'No.' The Major had a very brisk way of speaking. I would be sent for, and I wasn't to say a word about it to anyone.

I pointed out to him that you can't keep anything secret in the villages around Sandringham, and my mate Steele would know I'd been there whether I told him or not.

'Don't worry about that, Rush,' said the Major. Then the line went dead.

Even then it never occurred to me why I was being sent for. In due course the estate car came and whisked me away to Sandringham, through the back gate without the gatekeeper even nodding, to York Cottage, where Queen Mary gave birth to all her children before it was converted to offices.

Major Fellowes and his clerk Mr Pillar were waiting for me in a large room with a big fire and pictures of horses on all the walls. Both of them had quite recently come to Sandringham from somewhere round Oxford way, having worked together for years. The Major was the military-looking man I'd been expecting, tall and straight as a ramrod, with a clipped moustache, but he was wearing the tweeds and brogues of a country gentleman. Once I had a cup of coffee balanced on my knees, he produced a letter from the Queen asking if I would take over caring for her pigeons.

My first reaction was great surprise; my second was that the idea was impractical. I would have to ride my bike over to Sandringham twice a day to exercise the birds, train them, clean and feed them. On a Friday night I'd have to ride over to pick out the birds for the race that weekend. And there was the time I would need to spend with the birds if they were going to race home for me and win.

I knew the Royal Lofts well. They were in the village of West Newton, which is as close to Sandringham House as you can get without climbing over the red stone walls that shut off the grounds. There is a school in West Newton, a village school with a couple of rooms inside it and a little bell tower on top. A house somewhat larger than the school stands next to it – on a slight rise in the ground so that it seems even larger. The house was built by King George V for Mr Jones, the village schoolmaster. Mr Jones was a great friend of the King. People said they were like brothers, and in one sense they were: they both were pigeon fanciers. As well as being the village schoolmaster Mr Jones was the very first Royal Lofts manager, and the King built the Royal Lofts in Mr Jones's garden next to the house.

They were rather smart as lofts go, the Sandringham carpenters having their pick of the wood. There was an aviary like a huge Victorian birdcage, such as might be hung outside a parlour window on a fine day – except it was big enough for Mr Jones and his visitors to wander around in it. The quantity of wrought iron used in its construction would not have disgraced a seaside pier. The house had been given to someone else when Mr Jones died, and then the farm manager took it over, but the Lofts remained. I had wandered around in the aviary many a time with Steele, admiring the royal stock. If I were to take charge of the birds – and they were fine birds – I would want to spend a good many of my waking hours with them. A loft without a fancier in it day in and day out is a home without a heart for the birds. The racing pigeon is a rare bird in the compliment it pays the man who cares for it well – it will race home to him at astonishing speeds. But the fancier has to prove his devotion, and a smart loft alone won't hurry the bird home. With the Royal Lofts a good half-hour's bike ride away from where I lived in Gaywood, on the edge of King's Lynn, it would be hard going to give the birds the attention they all thrived on.

'I couldn't live out here in the country,' I told the Major. 'I wouldn't want to be so far away I couldn't even walk into Lynn, like I used to as a boy.'

'The Queen has weighed all that up, Rush,' the Major said.

It was hard to believe my ears, but I had, it seemed, been the subject of some thought on Her Majesty's part. Never having met the Queen I didn't know then what an eye she had for detail, both in what she sees around her and in considering a matter such as this. The Major put me straight.

'You're to keep your own birds, Rush,' he told me, 'and your own lofts. Build new ones next to them for the Queen's birds. You can choose whichever birds you want from the current lofts and dispose of the rest. That should set you up.'

I sat and thought for a moment. 'I still don't see how that would work,' I said.

'Indeed, why not?' he shot back.

I had to explain to him how complicated it would be. 'For a start,' I said, 'there would be two lots of corn, one for Her Majesty's birds and one for mine. People would soon begin to say old Len Rush is on the fiddle, getting free grub for his own birds.'

The Major stared at me as if I was a corporal about to lose my stripes, then he went back to reading the Queen's letter. 'You're to have complete freedom and complete control over all matters concerned with Her Majesty's racing pigeons, with no interference from anybody,' he said. 'You're to treat the royal birds exactly as if they were your own. Now what do you say?'

How could any flyer in the whole country say no to that? I would have to give up my own birds, I knew that straightaway, to protect my own name, but I couldn't say no to such an opportunity as the Queen herself had put in my way. What wouldn't I say to Steele when I next saw him!

2

My Beauty Boy Lenny

I'd had my heart set on racing pigeons since I was eight years old, when a bird with a ring on its leg came out of the sky to land on my bedroom window. I know it was spring and it was evening, and the bird stayed there two nights and the day between. I tried and I tried to get that bird, but it stayed out of my reach. I can see it now – it was a blue chequered bird, and from the shape of its head it must have been a cock. It was beautiful. I know a fancier who was so keen when he was a kid that he sold his first bike to buy a couple of racing pigeons. Once the idea was in my head I seemed to see pigeons everywhere that I'd never noticed before – the sky was full of them. But none of them were racing pigeons, none was like that bird; they were all wild. I suppose it was like wanting the moon, wanting the birds, but I had got so close to the bird on my windowsill.

That would have been in the second house we lived in. I was born where the village of Gaywood ends – only about two hundred yards from where I live now, though today it's surrounded by houses – in a cottage down Field Lane. It was one of a row of cottages called Rag Row because they were built by a rag and bone man. They were said to be built of shit and cinders. There was more than one field up the lane there, all owned by the Bagge family of Gaywood Hall, and one of them was the village playing field where we played football, one of the great loves of my life. I had been captain of the

19

Gaywood team for years when Lord Bagge died and the land was sold off as building plots. I scored the last two goals there.

When I was a boy my mother's parents lived on one side of the street in the village of East Winch and my Uncle Jim lived on the other side of the street. Both my parents were born there, about four miles outside Lynn, and they both went to school there. My father went quite young, in his early teens, to lodge with Ernie Loades, the blacksmith and undertaker of East Walton nearby. Ernie was in business with his brother Jimmy and between them they did all the carting on the roads, including the stones and gravel. They were looked after by their sister, who was the only woman in the house. My father intended to marry her. I don't know what happened, but what matters is that when his plans for Miss Loades fell through, my father married my mother instead.

My mother had four brothers: Herbert, who was a shepherd, Jim, Charlie and Will. My Uncle Jim once told me that Will said to him on my parents' wedding day, 'I think she's a bloody fool, 'cos if she hadn't had him nobody else would.' My father didn't mix with people, and his brothers and sisters didn't either – not even with each other. I hardly ever saw them when I was a child, whereas my uncles and my aunt on my mother's side were a regular part of our life. My Aunt Annie married a miner and moved away to Nottingham, but we'd go there and stay with her.

I once told the Queen I'd had the best mother and the best father anyone could possibly want, which is nothing but the truth. The difference between my parents and the way I felt about them was that my mother loved me and told me so, whereas I only found out how much my father cared for me after he was dead, when people told me how proud he had been of me. From when I was a boy I'd always believed he'd found me wanting. It was the way my mother loved me that made me such a happy child.

When I was five years old we moved about a mile away to

a house on the Wootton Road. There was a field on the other side of the road to us there which was where the night cart would be emptied every week. On a frosty night you would hear the old horse clumping along with his shoes on from miles away. In King's Lynn they had proper sewage pipes in those days, and in Gaywood they'd been on the sewer for years, but there were about two hundred yards between the two districts that weren't connected up to any pipes. People used pails instead of a lavatory, and the old night cart would go from house to house every Friday night to collect the contents. Our house was in the unplumbed part.

My very first clear memory is of water. On the day we moved I went down to the Wootton Road with my father to see the old Gatehouse that was to be our home. I remember my father opening the door, and inside from wall to wall was a sheet of water. The river had flooded. I suppose my parents managed to clear the water out and dry the place so it was fit for us to live in, but I only remember the water. The River Gaywood was at the end of our garden path. There was a plank going out into it, and one of my jobs was to walk along the plank, scrape the mud away from the end of it and stick a bucket into the water. That was what we and everyone else round about drank and used for everything else right up to the time we moved back to Gaywood ten years later. I don't remember my mother boiling the water much. I was a ruddy-faced little boy and thank God very healthy; the worst thing I ever had was diphtheria from drinking the river water.

Soon after we moved to the Gatehouse on the Wootton Road I started school – it was quite a mile away from home. My mother took me the first morning and I was lined up with all the other kiddies to sing 'There is a Green Hill Far Away'. That was a good start, because I loved to sing and I knew the hymn from chapel. But at the end of the morning I went that mile home to lunch then back to school on my own, and my mother never took me again. She didn't have time to walk to

Gaywood and back four times a day. I was on my own, and after the first half-hour I never much liked school. I liked it less each year I was there and the teachers seemed to think I was a proper duffer, but when it came time to leave, when I was fourteen, I didn't want to – because I was in the school football team. I loved playing football so much that I stayed on an extra term. From the earliest age I was mad about sport. Instead of sums and lessons, my school slate was always filled with pictures of goalkeepers making miraculous saves.

Not long after I started school the First World War began, and I remember looking at the sky and seeing Zeppelins. I spent many of my childhood days on the Reffley Farm where my father was foreman – he was marvellous with the animals. Because of the mutual respect between Jack Walden the vet and my father we would sometimes call in at his house in Albert Street, until one terrible day when a Zeppelin dropped a bomb on the house and destroyed it, along with all the outbuildings where there were animals.

On another occasion, my mother and I went to Highgate Chapel in the middle of the town for a tea one Saturday, and when we came out the road was filled with anti-aircraft guns and searchlights tearing along down to Sandringham to defend the King. Up in the sky were the Zeppelins, moving slowly in that direction. I would have clung to my mother like a baby, only she was frightened too. I have only bad memories of airships. When I was older the R-101, that later crashed in flames, came over, and the streets of Lynn were covered in oil from its passing.

There were just a few other children living close to us on the Wootton Road, the Howlett family of five girls that lived down the lane, Harry Collison who was my friend, and Benny and John Culey who lived up at the big house on Folly Farm. After the First World War a rag and bone man named Burrells came to live with his family in a ruin of a cottage on the top of the hill beyond Folly Farm. He walked with a terrible limp from a wound he had got in the War, and I remember the first time he came round looking for rags and bones he came with just a sack over his shoulder because he was so poor he didn't have a horse and cart. But he had five children and they were all unbelievably filthy. We called them Stinkerburrells, and no one would sit next to them in class.

The Culeys were fishing people from the North End and they had another house down there, Fair Lawn, where Mr and Mrs Culey would go every night, leaving the three children – the two boys and a girl, Edna, who wasn't right in the head – in the care of a servant named Woner (from his having only one arm) Catton. Harry Collison and I would go up to Folly Farm every evening – we had the run of the place – and when Mr Culey was there he would lay on all sorts of games for us. One Saturday he drove to the Wootton Road in a brand-new car to pick up his two sons and me. We went back to the North End – the car smelt of leather, like a football – parked the car beside Fair Lawn, then went on foot to the Walks ground to watch Lynn play Walthamstow Avenue. I was nine years old, and that was the very first football match I went to.

Mrs Culey came with us to see her brother play. She was a member of the old Chase family, fishing people from the North End, and there was nearly always a Chase in the Lynn team – they were just as famous for football as for cockles. Her brother had been out on the cockling grounds in the morning, as usual – the boat had gone out into the Wash until it reached the sands, then waited for the tide to go out and leave the boat high and dry. There would be water all around to the horizon except for these islands of sand where the boat was stranded. Everyone had a little rake with nails stuck in it for raking up the cockles before the tide came in again. Then the footballing Chase had been put ashore just this side of Hunstanton, and he'd walked more than ten miles to be at the Walks ground for the kick-off at two-thirty in the afternoon.

Mr Culey got richer and richer over the years; he was a

marvellous businessman, though I don't know if he could tell an A from a B. He bought up a lot of land just before the Second World War, then sold the lot to the RAF for the Marham aerodrome to be built there. He hd a yacht that was bigger than the Queen's. When Edna grew up he got a man to marry her and put them into a smallholding at Middleton, but the fellow didn't realise what a good opportunity it was and he was never happy. Then in later years Mr Culey would take the whole of the Lynn team up to Wembley for an international match, treating the lot of them – including me, at that time. And one day he came up to me and said, 'Here you are, Rushy, you can have this. I had a good deal in London today.' He handed me a huge silver bowl that was worth £84 in those days. It stayed in my wardrobe for years until I got Walthamstow Avenue to come and play for it. It's called the Culey Cup, and it's been played for ever since.

My father was never a football man – in fact he hated it. His great skill was with animals, and it was shortly after we moved to the Gatehouse on the Wootton Road that he became foreman on the Reffley Farm. Before that he had been plate-layer on the Midland and Great Northern – the Gatehouse belonged to the railway company. The reason my father was glad to move there was that two fields and various farm buildings went with the house, and he added to the buildings so that he could keep pigs in comfort.

My father loved keeping pigs. He had all the butcher's utensils. At the beginning of winter a man by the name of Rudd would come from Grimstone to our house to kill the pigs. I kept out of the way. Rudd would set a huge vat of water boiling on a stove, then hold the pig on a big old stool to kill it, after which it was dumped whole in the boiling water. It would be scraped and cleaned when it was taken from the water, then cut up, hung and salted. Some was sold and some we kept. We always had a good table, even though my father didn't have two halfpennies to rub together then. When he sold the meat from his first pig he had to pay back the corn merchant, Mr Rust, in Lynn, because all the food that had made the pig fat for killing had been got on tick from him. My father had to get grub for the pig on tick once or twice, but after that he was able to pay for it, and after the first year he always had more than one pig.

There's no doubting my father was shrewd, and all his life he worked hard. It was all that mattered – work, work, work. And he expected me to help out from when I was just a little tot – he had an allotment as well as the fields by the house where he would take me and set me to work weeding the onions and jobs like that. I hated it.

Mr Playford was lucky to get him as foreman for the Reffley Farm, and the luck worked both ways because we were better off after that. But I had the most luck of all from the arrangement because Mr Playford treated me like the son he'd never had, and unlike my father Mr Playford enjoyed just the things I did. He was a great cricketer. He took me to Wisbech when the great Jack Hobbs came to open the ground. Hobbs couldn't get there for that day, but in the evening, when Mr Playford and I were at the station to get the train back to King's Lynn, Hobbs was just arriving. I saw him get out of the train but he was rushed away from the platform – so I went and sat in the very seat he'd travelled in, while it was still warm. Mr Playford bought me some cricket boots and a lovely sweater which I've still got now, over seventy years later.

He was quite new to farming. Until he took over the Reffley Farm he'd been Alfred Playford, master baker from Burnham Market. He was a small man, very neat, and with a little fair moustache and the loveliest sense of humour – you could see it in his face; but he'd set his heart on being a farmer, so he rented the farm from Sir Everard Foulkes, the owner, and moved with his wife to the farmhouse. Back in Burnham Market he left his three daughters, Grace, Maud and Blanche, to run the bakery. It was a big bakery serving all seven Burnhams:

Burnham Sutton, Burnham Deepdale, Burnham Overy, Burnham Weskett, Burnham Thorpe, Burnham Norton and Burnham Market itself. The new farm supplied feed for all the horses that used to pull the bread carts. Clover and hay were all baled up and every week my father would take a double-breasted wagon harnessed with two horses the twenty-five miles to Burnham Market.

The first time I ever went in a railway carriage, I went alone to meet my father in Burnham Market and drove back to the farm with him in the empty cart – I was about eight. I went on the King's Lynn to Hunstanton line, and I had to change at Heacham. From there I caught the Heacham and Wells-next-the-Sea line which passes through Burnham Market – or at least it did until Mr Beeching axed it. That was the start of my love of travelling by train.

I stayed in Burnham Market for the day. Grace, Maud and Blanche were at the bakery in Front Street: Grace ran the house above the bakery, while the other two girls worked on the bakers' carts. The stables where my father had brought the cart were next to the shop. Nearby was a very old pub called the Host Arms, run by two boys, Harold and Royal, and their mother, Mrs Womac. Grace was courting Royal.

Blanche was the one who made a real fuss of me. She was a wonderful artist – beautiful country scenes she painted, that were hung all over the farmhouse in gilt frames. She was courting a lovely man named Frank Barnsdall, the son of a schoolmaster at Wallasey in Cheshire, across the Mersey, but somehow Mr Playford never liked him. Frank would come and stay at the farmhouse for weekends, and it was obvious to everyone that Mr Playford had taken against him. I don't know why, because Frank was a very nice chap. He and I would go fishing together – he bought me a rod and all the different hooks.

Most weekends Mr and Mrs Playford went to Burnham Market to see how the business was going on, but they would never leave the farmhouse empty, so Mum, Father and I would live up at the farmhouse those weekends. I was given the bedroom facing the Wootton Road. The first night we went there I looked out of the window and I saw moving lights going along, so I rushed into my parents' bedroom. They explained that what I was seeing were the lights of passing motor cars.

My mother worked in the dairy at the farm, and she did the housework in the farmhouse for Mrs Playford. Milking began at five-thirty in the morning, then my mother would come back to the house to get me off to school while my father took the milk cart into Lynn with the big churns on it. On my way home from school, the milk cart would sometimes overtake me along the Wootton Road and I'd get a lift up to the farm. One time, Mr Playford was driving it and he passed me – I was with my friend from school, Muriel Sylvester, who lived even further along the road than I did. She had lovely golden hair, and as we walked along she had her arm round my neck. Mr Playford called out to us, and Muriel, being cheeky, told him, 'Len says he loves me.' It was terrible. Of course I knew he'd tell my mother when he saw her. I'd already been in trouble for writing a love letter to another girl with long golden hair named Queenie Hampton. My mother saw the letter and she said. 'God doesn't love boys that do that,' which scared the life out of me. But Mr Playford must have made it into a joke, because I wasn't told I would go to hell for it. Mr Playford was always pulling my leg. My mother would call me her 'beauty boy Lenny', and he did too. He always called me Lenny or Leonard, never Len like everyone else.

The missus didn't fuss over me so much. She was a short woman, but so heavy she would surprise you by the quick-footed way she moved about – not that she wouldn't be out of breath from the effort. And she would drink so, like her sister Mrs Griffin. Mrs Griffin lived next door to a pub in Gaywood (it's a Chinese restaurant now), and she'd be in and out, in and out – she used to drink like anything. It got so bad that Mr Griffin had to take her away from there, to Middleton. Mrs Playford would buy a couple of bottles of whisky every market day, then she would get my father to buy her a bottle when he went into Lynn with the milk cart. I don't know as Mr Playford was aware of the errands my father did for his wife, but my father was a hard man. If Mrs Playford wanted to drink herself to death, that wasn't his concern. One night we were sitting at home and there was a knock on the back door. My father went to answer it and there was Mrs Playford. She'd set out to go to Burnham Market and got on the wrong train because she was boozed – she'd been to Downham, which is in the opposite direction. Now she wanted my father to give her a lift home, which he did without a word.

My father kept a pony and trap in one of the outbuildings – we had a marvellous pony named Pippin which my father was always being asked to sell. He was a chestnut, glossy as you like, and the trap was very smart, with rubber tyres and lamps on it. We would drive out to East Winch at the weekends to visit my mother's family. We lived very quiet lives: that either my father or my mother should ever be the worse for drink was unthinkable. My parents would go to chapel every Sunday, and I would go to Sunday school. Every other Monday night my father went to the Gaywood Adult School Sick and Dividing Club, of which he was treasurer. He was very friendly with Mr Darken the milkman, who was chairman of the club, and old Reeve the roadman, who was the secretary. If you belonged to the club you would get ten bob a week whenever you were ill. But apart from that he never went out of a night-time, and my mother went out even less. As far as I was aware most people were like that in those days. People were more content. At home my father read the newspaper, while my mother knitted and mended our clothes.

But the Playfords were different. They enjoyed a good time, and they never missed an opportunity to lay on a feast and a party for their friends. I was different, too, being just a boy. I was always out, at the chapel youth club or playing football. A chap came to Gayood and started a scout club. I was at that for three or four weeks, then just as we started to learn knots we were told that we had to have a uniform, and that was the end of it for me: my mother and father couldn't afford a uniform. But I found other reasons for being out at night, like going up to Folly Farm with Harry Collison. I had to be home early, of course. I would run home, and my poor mother would come along the road to meet me because she was worried. 'Here's my beauty boy Lenny,' she would say, and it was always nice to see her.

My father would never come along the road to meet me or anything like that. He was Victorian, stern, honest and straight as a gun. Not once did he hit me – which must say something about him, considering the hidings kids got in those days – but he would shout at me, tell me not to do things, tell me playing football and cricket was a waste of time. He was set on a life of work, and it was a great relief to me as a boy to be with someone like Mr Playford or Frank Barnsdall.

Grace Playford never married Mrs Womac's son from the Host Arms in Burnham Market. She never married at all, and none of the girls married until late in life. Maud, the eldest, married an ironmonger from Fakenham, and Blanche married Frank. On both occasions Mr and Mrs Playford put up a huge tent on the front lawn of the farmhouse, with a lovely wood floor for dancing, all polished. Outside, all the carriages were lined up to take the guests the mile from the farmhouse to the church. There were some motor cars too, I suppose, but I never took much notice of them. I sat on the front of the biggest old coach, next to the driver.

The first time I ever went into a theatre was with the Playford girls. They took me to a pantomime in Lynn one Boxing Day afternoon when I was about seven years old. Maud was a bit snobbish about it. I was only the humble son of humble workers, and the people Maud mixed with were far superior to me and my father and mother. She was one of the people that entertained, that was the big distinction, and young as I was I grasped this.

From the time we lived on Rag Row I had been going each Christmas to Gaywood Hall where the Bagges, the brewing family, entertained everyone who lived under them. It's not a beautiful house, just a big Victorian pile of flint and brick all squared off and solid-looking. All the kids from Gaywood went there. I've still got a lovely wooden steam engine that they gave me one Christmas – there was always a great big fire going in the ballroom with a tree all lit up and Father Christmas next to it, doling out the most beautiful presents from a huge sack.

Lord and Lady Bagge had either four or five daughters. The other big family of the village, the Radcliffes, had daughters too, and I only remember that between them the Bagges and the Radcliffes had nine daughters, and no sons. The Radcliffes lived in the rectory because he was an archdeacon. The rectory wasn't as big as the Hall, but the Radcliffes were said to be richer. Mrs Radcliffe was a Boer, and her family had made a fantastic fortune from diamond mines in South Africa. The church in Gaywood has a beautiful carved pulpit in oak presented by Mrs Radcliffe. She also gave a new stained glass window and paid for no end of repairs.

There was an ornamental pool in front of Gaywood Hall, and the grass stretching down to it from the front of the house was the village cricket pitch where I played for years. All the children of the village had a feeling that the Hall was part of their lives, because we were allowed to play in the park in the evening of a summertime. We could treat the place like our own back yard until seven o'clock, when the Hall bell went for dinner. Then off, and woe betide anybody who so much as touched the branch of a tree after that time. It was reported to school next morning, and you'd be for it.

As a child I understood that the Bagges were above the Playfords in the scheme of things, and on the same level as the Bagges were the Foulkes family of Hillington. Sir Everard Foulkes owned the Reffley Farm and two other big farms thereabouts. He used the Reffley Farm for shooting parties. All the gentlemen he knew would gather there, and myself and all the local boys would act as beaters for them, tramping through the undergrowth to flush out pheasants for the gentry.

I went to school with the two sons of the gamekeeper for the Bagge estate, a man by the name of Hall. He was friendly, which is not a word I would use for all the keepers I knew when I was a boy. He was a big, strong, ex-army man, and his wife was a frail little woman who gave him two sons his own size. As well as being a keeper, Mr Hall kept a pub right in the middle of a wood near Middleton station – it was called the Eel's Toe, which I thought was a good joke even as a child. I loved going there to play with the boys. There were sandpits close by that have been getting bigger and bigger ever since – all those years a trainload of sand has been taken from them every working day.

The keeper for our part of Sir Everard's estate was Harry Bridges. He was terrifying, and I never dared go into the Reffley Woods for fear of him. The Reffley Temple was there, a place of great mystery to me as a boy. Set above a spring of continuous flowing water, it was a lovely old ornamental building, not meant to be lived in, with a very tall monument in front of it and a twelve-foot diameter bowl at the monument's base into which the spring ran. Two stone lions stood guard over it.

I would sometimes catch sight of Sir Everard when he came down to the Reffley Temple to attend meetings of the Reffley Brethren. The Brethren would gather at the Temple perhaps twice a year to drink a special punch and smoke tobacco in pipes that were twelve inches long. The punch had a secret recipe, and in those days only two men knew it: Mr Aubrey

Ram, the Conservative agent, and Sir Basil Humphrey. Around the walls inside the Temple were photographs of the Brethren of days gone by, most of the lords of the area and other big landowners that didn't have titles. There were about forty Brethren when I was a boy. A meal would be laid on for them and in summer they would play bowls on the grass in front of the Temple, although it wasn't very good for playing on. Aubrey Ram was also our cricket captain and he said to me once, 'I would love to make you a member of the Brethren, but you don't drink, so I can't invite you,' and that was the end of that.

But the Reffley Woods were out of bounds. Everywhere was so secret when I was a boy. You weren't allowed on to other people's land like you are now, and it was different also because there were far more people on the land. When I go to see a farmer friend of mine today I'll see perhaps one man working in a field during the whole day. When I was a boy working people were part of the landscape like the hawthorn trees in a hedge: men and horses, living creatures working the land. And a great deal of that land is built on now. The Bagges' land is gone – I built my own house on a patch of it in 1936 – and the grounds of the Hall have been carved up for lines of bungalows. The Reffley Farm is now the Reffley Estate – a housing estate.

It was a big farm of about six hundred acres. The farmyard was huge, paved all over with bricks. The riding stables ran along one side of it, and to the left of the house was the dairy where my mother worked. There were stacks all around the yard, and a big brick barn, a cow house, the cart shed, the turnip house, the cake house – all sorts of outbuildings. I remember the time when the cow house floor was concreted. I had an old horse named Beauty I had to take with the tumble right through what we called the top meadows, the last three meadows at the end of the farm, through a wood to a barn that was broken down. I collected all the old bricks and rubble from the barn to make the foundations for the concrete. What would be done now in one day with a JCB and a skip on a lorry took me the whole of my Easter holidays. One day I ran over a snake about three feet long when I was going backwards and forwards with the tumble through the meadows and the wood. Today it is covered by houses and a Co-op supermarket.

3

Figures in the Landscape

I worked on the farm from the age of eight until I left school at fourteen. Directly school ended I would go and turn the handle on the old butter churn for my mother. Almost everyone would take a turn on that handle, even Mrs Playford. You would turn and turn the handle and the milk would go to cream and then all of a sudden it would be butter. Sometimes my mother would put some liquid into the butter to make it yellow.

There would be odd jobs to do in the yard or outbuildings, cleaning up, and dogs and the chickens to feed. There were two dogs living in the farmyard, a lovely old Scotch terrier named Prince and a vicious mongrel that didn't have a name, unless it was one of the curses people threw at it. Every time it saw you it would try to bite you.

Prince was a great favourite of a baker named Mr Riddout from North End. Mr Riddout would come to the farm on a Wednesday evening, say, to shoot rabbits, and he always took Prince with him. I also would go with him, but I think I probably invited myself along. I've never once in my life fired a gun myself, but I loved being out. The sky could be so beautiful at that time of day – a really big sky over the saltmarshes and the sea, with hardly a tree poking into it. Rabbits would scatter in every direction at our approach. When I went out to the fens on my own I would go quietly and then the rabbits didn't move. They were busy eating or sniffing the breeze: thousand upon thousand pairs of ears standing upright above the grass, as if someone had carefully put them there, one pair of ears for so many square feet of eatables.

But going with Prince and Mr Riddout was a different matter. The dog was an enthusiast. He didn't take himself seriously like some dogs do. He didn't blot out the rest of the world once the smell of rabbit hit his nose. He wanted to share the wonder of it, bounding backwards and forwards like a team leader, inspiring Mr Riddout and me to take the whole of the rabbit kingdom by storm. Mr Riddout thought Prince was grand, being a hearty bloke himself. Once he was shooting rabbits out in the whin bushes on the fens when Prince happened to be chasing the same rabbit that Mr Riddout was aiming to shoot. The rabbit got away, but poor little Prince was peppered with shot. The brown spots on his white coat were changed by that, but Prince stayed the same. He should have been dead, for the shot got him full on.

Saturday mornings I had various jobs up at the farmhouse. Covering the front door was a big verandah with a circular window in it. I had to get up there and clean the glass, and then I had to clean all the knives and forks. After that I'd go round the farmyard collecting all the eggs from the chickens and ducks. Sometimes the grass growing between the bricks in the yard and round the edges would get untidy, and I'd have to cut it out. I hated working on that. The biggest job was mucking out the stables. There were so many horses of all sorts – Arabs, Shires, Suffolks. There were riding horses and carthorses, ponies and hunters. Mr Playford loved hunting, and he always rode his favourite named Queenie to the hunt. One weekend when he and Mrs Playford were in Burnham Market the stable lad rode Queenie, jumped a gate and broke her leg. The poor creature had to be destroyed, and everyone was in a great stew over what to tell Mr Playford when he got back. But he was never angry; he was such a nice bloke that it was terrible to see him upset.

When I'd mucked out the stables I had to sweep the whole yard clean and have all the straw cleared up ready for Sunday. As far as I know neither Mr nor Mrs Playford ever went to church, but they were very particular to have everything spick and span for Sunday. I had a barrow with a dustbin to take all the muck and dirt out into a field and spread it on the land.

When I was older, another of my Saturday jobs was to take the horses to the blacksmith in South Wootton. I'd take whichever horse needed new shoes. Mystery, Flirt, Prince, Gypsy, Diamond, Bounce, Captain ... they all had names, but there were so many I can't remember every one of them. Prince was a carthorse. He would have pulled down a church, he really would. Flirt was the only one you had to be careful of; he must have been ill-treated at some time because he would try very hard to bite you when he was being put in the shafts. It was Mystery I learned to ride on. She was a riding horse but a sort of half strain with a pony, a docile old horse, brown all over. For some reason she was always afraid of the men who went up the telegraph poles. I took her to the blacksmith's once, which was about a mile and a half away, and I had strict orders to get off if I found myself approaching a telegraph pole with a man up it. As I turned a corner in the road, there was a man up a telegraph pole. The next thing I knew I was waking up in the farmhouse. The horse had just stood there once she'd thrown me off, and the men had come and carried me back.

Mr Playford fell out with Mr Blake, the first blacksmith I went to at South Wootton, although he was a good blacksmith. He had a much older man working for him, old Sam Finn. There was a pub, the New Inn, right next door to Blake's forge, and the old boy would be backwards and forwards, especially on hot days. I used to pump the bellows for him and throw water on the wheel rims to cool them. There was a wheelwright's shop adjoining, and I'd go into it because there was a cricket bat in there, one that Mr Blake had made. It was only a shaped piece of wood, but I played and played with that cricket bat and eventually Mr Blake let me have it.

Then Mr Playford transferred his business to the Gaywood blacksmith, Stan Nichols. Stan knew I was mad on football and he used to save me the photographs of players from Pinnace cigarettes. I've got them even now. Stan was a big chap, terrifically strong, whereas Mr Blake was a shortish, oldish, thin man.

I'd go crow-scaring when the corn was planted, which was a very monotonous job once I'd finished building myself a shelter in the corner of a field. But when harvest time came round I would work from dawn till dusk every day and there was nothing at all boring about it. When the day came that the corn was ripe, my mother and father and two other men would go all around the edge of a field with hand scythes, cutting a swathe wide enough to get a binding machine into the field – three carthorses pulled the binding machine, two on the middle shaft and the third on the outside, which was loose. No matter how strong they were, the horses on the middle shaft needed a rest every ten rounds or so, and the outside horse would swop places with one of the others.

Somehow or other Harry Bridges, the gamekeeper, always had an idea when we'd got to the last two rounds of cutting the corn. Some of the rabbits would remain in the corn until the very last and the men would shoot them as they came bucketing out. Harry was there in case any pheasants were flushed out along with the rabbits, to watch that they weren't shot as well. I thought it was strange how he always knew the right time to appear in the field.

Once the corn was cut I went on what was called the hold-ye, which was sitting on the horses in the shafts as they went from shuck to shuck to be loaded up. There were two men on the back of the cart, and if you didn't give them warning they could fall off. I had to call out, 'Hold-ye!' If I didn't they wouldn't half swear at me. The loads would get very high; to get down the men would have to drive a pitchfork into the load and swing down to the ground on it.

The next move was to drive the cart fully loaded to the stackyard, which could be half a mile away. There were competitions to see who had the best stackyard, and quite an amount of jealousy amongst farmers over the propping that had to be done – propping denotes bad stacking. The bottom was made from branches of thorn trees and bushes to keep the stack off the ground. Then an elevator was set up beside it – a platform with a long arm underneath which was attached to a big cogwheel – and inside the wheel was a horse going round and round, poor thing. Every time I left a field with a fully loaded cart, the men would say, 'And mind you don't hit those bloody gateposts!' because it was a narrow gate into the yard and I would need my wits about me to get the cart through.

After that there was horse-raking to pick up all the gleanings. That was another great thrill, to be in charge of the rake horse. There was a seat on the rake with a big handle beside it and I'd go bumping up and down the field behind the horse to make a long row of corn across the end of the field by pulling up the handle.

When I went on the horse-raking I did what they called the full harvest, about a month's work. Mr Playford was a very generous man to me. He might go a month without giving me a sausage, and then he would give me £3 10s, which was a fortune in those days. I saved it. I was always a saver. My father gave me money for the jobs I did for him, and I didn't waste it. We had a postman named Jimmy Gardener, and when he came round he would sing out: 'Post! Post!' One day he said to my mother, 'Have you registered that boy in the Post Office Savings?' My mother said she hadn't, so Jimmy said, 'Well, I think he ought to be. I'll give him sixpence to start off.' So he gave me my first sixpence, and by the time I was fourteen I think I had something around £18 saved up, which was a tremendous lot of money.

When the last cartload of corn was squeezed between the

gateposts and the space in the stackyard was filled with the stacks like great yellow buildings (which the rats would soon be living in, by the thousand), everyone felt how good it was to have done all that. If there was a chance of getting the harvest home before the sun went down everyone worked twice as hard to finish that day rather than the next, finishing in the last of the sunset.

Then there was harvest supper in the barn. The whole place was lit with hurricane lamps hanging from the rafters. There wasn't a mournful face to be seen if the harvest had been halfway good. Nor was there a pale face, everyone having been in the open all the hours of daylight, burned by the sun and fit from all the effort. Plates heaped with roast beef and gravy were set before us to eat. Everyone was so hungry that there was quiet to begin with, but there was beer for the men to drink, so the quiet didn't last long. There were mountains of fresh bread and puddings from the bakery in Bunham Market, and Grace, Maud, Blanche and Mrs Griffin would be there, ready for a good time. When no one could eat any more, it would be time to start the singing.

I like to remember Mr Playford as he was on those occasions. No one enjoyed themselves more than he did, and he was a lovely man. That might have been part of his problem, because he wasn't a good farmer. He would treat his men well, but they would rule him, some of them – he just couldn't bring himself to be hard. He didn't even sack the stable lad that broke his favourite hunter's leg. There was one occasion at threshing time, just before Christmas, when the pile of coal Mr Playford had got in for the stream-driven threshing engine started going down much quicker than the engine was using it. The village policeman was sent for, and he found the missing coal. The man was taken to the station, but Mr Playford didn't press charges – he just took the loss.

And Mr Playford's luck was terrible, like with his horse breaking her leg. There was always some horse or cow falling into the dyke and drowning – everything went wrong for him. He was lucky to have my father as foreman, because my father was his opposite and what success the farm had was owing to that. But it wasn't enough. One night Mrs Playford broke her leg walking across the farmyard. Two doctors, their regular Dr De Mere and his brother, came to set the leg up in Mrs Playford's bedroom the same night. She had no end of operations on it – it cost Mr Playford a fortune in hospital bills, but it never healed.

When I reached fourteen and it was time to start work in earnest my father said nothing about me deciding to stay on at school an extra term, although I'm sure he knew why I was staying on. But when I did leave I didn't tell him in so many words why it was I didn't want to go on the farm, which seemed the obvious choice for me since I'd loved working there after school and through the holidays. As far as I was concerned farm work was out of the question – farm workers didn't stop work until three o'clock of a Saturday afternoon, and kick-off at the Lynn ground was always at two-thirty.

If I wasn't going to work on the land, my father wanted me to be a butcher's boy – I could have worked with a friend of his who came to Lynn as a slaughterer. He and my father had known each other all their lives, they'd been to school together in East Winch, and now they're buried within six feet of each other in the Gaywood Cemetery. My father said there's no poor butcher's boy, but I didn't want to be a butcher. I couldn't do the killing – butchers in those days had to turn live animals into meat to sell. It had been quite natural when I was a boy to hit and kill rabbits when they were flushed out of a harvest field, but I could no more do that now than fly, and by the time I was fourteen I didn't have it in me to kill a living thing. It's the same with pigeons – except for the squabs that aren't formed right, for which drowning in a bucket seems the right thing to do. But I couldn't kill a grown bird. I might have been a gamekeeper because the life would have suited me –

43

except for the shooting and killing they have to do.

Then all of a sudden my father got me an apprenticeship in the building trade and I said, 'All right.' Billy Hill, the builder, was an ex-Lynn football player, and he had a mate of his working for him, George Monument, who had also played for the town – the company I would keep for five years as an apprentice suited me. And that's how I became a carpenter.

4

A Sport for Gentle Folk

I didn't inherit my father's natural ability with animals. He had a sixth sense about pregnant animals and the mothers and small ones when they were first born. One time the vet gave him half a crown for being right about what ailed a particular horse in foal; my father said the unborn foal was dead. The vet went away, then came back again for the birth, and when my father proved himself to be correct he gave him the money. But the whole business upset me. It was the same when the bull was put in with the cows, or when the stallion came to serve the mares. There was a farmer named Betts of Babbingly, which adjoins Sandringham, who would go all round Norfolk for weeks on end and wait outside various pubs for the farmers to book his stallion. When Mr Playford booked him to come and serve the mares on the Reffley Farm I had to be somewhere else because I couldn't bear to look at it going on.

But with birds it was different. I was never squeamish about the mating of my pigeons, otherwise I should never have got started. The subject of breeding is always uppermost in a flyer's thoughts. It's the breeding of winners a man has in mind when he sets up a loft in his back garden, the prospect of what he fancies in a bird being enhanced in the next generation and the next. I would watch with great interest the mating antics of my birds, to be sure that the eggs that later appeared in the nest bowl contained just the mix of blood I had in mind.

Racing pigeons are famously loyal to their mates, but there are, so to speak, some bad eggs amongst them. And they have arranged marriages, arranged by the fancier, which means they will be expected to change mates when the fancier sees fit. I wouldn't say I'd ever seen a pigeon heartbroken by this, but a pigeon will never ask for a divorce if it's left to itself. It's breeding as much as racing that holds the flyer. A flyer will always prefer to hold back a champion bird for breeding rather than send it off after another cup, once it has proved itself over distance. The thought of losing such a bird in a race will make him go cold in the night.

I built my first lofts when I was about seventeen, which meant I had already been wanting my own birds for more than half my life, since that stray pigeon landed on my bedroom windowsill. By this time I was an apprentice joiner. I still rode old Mystery out to the fens every morning first thing, to take a tumble full of chaff to the bullocks and the unbroken horses that Mr Playford kept out there. I would have to count the bullocks in case one had fallen into the water overnight. I went along an old railway line that was once built to join up King's Lynn with the Midland Railway going to Norwich. As far as I can remember there was never a train on it. The sleepers and the lines were put down, but then nothing happened and they were taken up again. When I rode along it only the posts at each side of the line were still there, but it was raised above the meadows and all the animals would watch me coming and follow to where I pitched out the food. The frost on some of the cow cabbages on a winter's morning at dawn was enough to take the palms of your hands off – some of them were so huge it was like lifting a block of ice the size of an armchair. But the cattle soon got to the middle of them: when I threw out mangels and turnips I'd cut into chips for them in the turnip house, the whole lot would have disappeared before I started back along the railway line. I carried on doing this long after I left school, because I was always awake in the early morning and there was nothing indoors to match being out at the beginning of the day. I was like my father in that.

But after my father bought his own house in Gaywood, I often didn't have time to go all the way from there to the Reffley Farm to feed the animals in the mornings, so little by little I stopped doing it. This, together with football in the evenings, made my father think I wasted a terrible lot of time. And on Saturday I would regularly spend at the cinema fivepence of the sixpence my mother gave me out of my apprentice's wages of 5s. I remember the lovely serials at the cinema – 'The Mysterious Airman' and 'The Green Archer'. The penny I had left I would spend on *The Pink 'Un*, which was a football paper from Norwich.

Then I met a wood machinist named John Richardson, and to my delight he was a champion flyer. When he moved from the little fishing cottage he lived in at North End he had to get rid of his birds, because there wasn't room to keep racing pigeons in his new back yard. He was going to take up show birds – none of your truly fancy birds like pouters or fantails, but show homers and racers that were bred for their looks rather than their performance and could be kept in the space he had. He knew I was very keen, so he gave me two of his very best birds.

One of them was a King's Cup winner named Bad Luck. It had flown the race from Lerwick in the Shetlands, 515 miles, 90 of them over water, which pigeons detest, to win the King George V Cup for the Midland section of the North Road Championship. The other was a beautiful blue bar hen by the name of Baldwin, to breed with Bad Luck. I've got the loft books even now where I put down what I bred from them. The books are all spattered with dung and stuck with bits of straw from being in the loft. My writing is just a boy's, and you can tell I had never been much interested in school. But when the Queen asked me to take over the royal pigeons I had birds in my loft that were the direct descendants of Bad Luck and Baldwin. Over the years I had sent several of them to the same race from Lerwick, and one of them had won the King's Cup for me.

At first I was content to breed from Baldwin and Bad Luck and train the young birds. I would pester John Richardson for tips on how to do it and how to keep the birds healthy, and the thrill of having the birds return from wherever they'd been tossed was enough to be getting on with. I would strap them in a basket on the front of my bike to take them on a mystery ride along country roads very early in the morning. Birds love the early morning. The very first thing I do every day and have done for the last sixty-odd years is to go down to my lofts and tend to the birds. I always said good morning to the birds before I said good morning to my wife Gladys.

There are hundreds of species of pigeons spread all over the surface of the world, wherever there's a morsel of food to be had, but whether it's a pure white dove or a tattered old street pigeon from Bangkok, there's one thing all pigeons have in common: they're not shy of man. I've heard of a bright green pigeon, which I would love to see, that lives in the forested mountains of Burma – uninhabited mountains until the Second World War, when the Japanese marched through from one direction and the British marched through from the other. The two armies clashed head on right where the pigeons had lived undisturbed since time began. But the pigeons kept to their roosts and took no account of the deafening noise and the smoke. Even at his fire and brimstone worst, man can't scare off pigeons.

The racing pigeon, however, is special, a thoroughbred, and it has to consent not only to live with man but to be handled by him. The rough-handed flyer will scare away a racing pigeon, or at least scare it out of reach. Imagine the frustration of a flyer when his birds refuse to come in after a race, preferring to sit on the roof of the loft after five hundred miles in the air than to be handled so that the race ring can be removed and put into the clock. Many a race has been lost by birds failing to trap quickly. Worse, many a bird has been lost to the wild by rough handling as a youngster or on its return from a race. You might say that pigeon racing is entirely a sport for gentle folk, because if you're not gentle and considerate in your behaviour towards the birds they will soon tell you so and go off in a huff.

The first place I ever took my birds for them to try their luck getting home again was Castle Rising, a distance of five miles, which I was told was about the right distance for a young bird's first experience of the basket. I had to keep Baldwin and Bad Luck prisoners because otherwise they would insist on flying back to the North End in search of John Richardson, but when their first chicks had taught themselves to fly the time came to make a test of the homing instinct their parents were famous for. There were two youngsters, and they had already been exercised around the loft for a couple of weeks twice a day after a light feed, so that half an hour or so of strenuous flying brought on a sharp hunger. For the purpose of calling them in again, I rattled a tin can with some corn in it. The birds get to know the sound of corn rattling in the can from when they first feed themselves, and it's a good sound, reminding them of food and home comforts – the birds will swoop from the sky back to their loft and the man with the tin can. After tossing the birds into the sky at Castle Rising I had to pelt home on my bike again to be there in the garden with the tin can rattling a welcome for them.

The next week I took them to Dersingham, a distance of eight miles. This was another village that more or less belongs to the royal estate; there are about nine of them in all – the village of Sandringham itself, West Newton, Fring, Hillington, Sherbourne, Castle Rising, Dersingham, Flitcham and Amner. From riding around on my bike as a boy I knew every acre of land on the Sandringham estate outside the walls around the house itself. I'd known much of the area since I was a small child

because my Uncle Herbert, my mother's youngest brother, was
a shepherd there. He worked for a farmer named Marshall
from North Lynn who farmed on the estate at Amner, and
sometimes I went there to stay for a week with my uncle and
aunt. I would go with him in his horse and cart to sit in the
sheep folds. I remember the first time I went to stay there was
a lamp on the table in the house. We had never had one at
home, and when I touched the glass I jerked my hand away
again, screaming and crying, for the unexpected heat had burnt
the skin from the palm of my hand and my fingers.

Castle Rising was my favourite village – one of the best in
the country, I would say. On one side of the church there are
no windows from the time when the sea came right in over
the Wolferton Marshes up to its walls. We all learnt the story
of Castle Rising when we were children in school, because no
end of people died there during the Black Death. They stayed
in the old church, which is a ruin now, rather than spread the
plague, and they all died there. Then in later years, although the
village was hardly bigger than a hamlet, it had two Members of
Parliament, one of whom was Sir Robert Walpole. With the
ruin of the castle sitting on top of its earthworks it was always
the most exciting place to go when I was a boy, especially with
my pigeons.

Each time I took the birds further and further away from
home. For their third flight I bumped them over the roads all
the way to Hunstanton – sixteen miles – and I would take
them there more than once, sometimes half a dozen times. I
would watch how after the first couple of flights they didn't
bother to circle in the sky and confer with each other, but just
bolted straight for home, getting there long before I ever did.

I only found out after the First World War was over why
it was that at that time I had searched in vain for a kit of racing
pigeons in the sky. I'd been too young at the time to understand,
but of course they had been banned for fear that spies would
use them. The only racing pigeons flying were those enlisted

by the Services, and although they used a great many it was nothing like the numbers of birds that are kept for pleasure in peacetime. I read the most heroic stories of birds used at the Battle of the Somme, flying to mobile lofts behind the front from where the battle was going on, over the barbed wire. In England lofts all along the east coast round to Hastings in the south had birds fit and ready to carry the news of an invasion, should it happen. What really amazed me was that birds had been regularly taken out on the high seas to relay messages home from the trawlers engaged in minesweeping. They had been dropped from planes countless times, often over water as the aircraft was being brought crashing down – and they dread water.

John Richardson had told me when he gave me the birds that King's Lynn was one of the worst places in the country for flying from the north because of its coastal situation. Rather than go across the Wash pigeons will add miles to their flight by going around it across the flats of Lincolnshire, sometimes as far as Spalding, before turning east to home. But if I was to race the birds I knew I would have to fly the North Road, as flyers in Lynn always have. I had a mate named Tubby Massingham who was the son of a captain on a boat belonging to the Boneses, the big fishing family. They were all sailboats – smacks – in those days, and if the tide or the wind was against them they had to row home. Tubby's father was dead set against Tubby joining him on the boat because of the hard life and the risk of losing him to the sea, so Tubby had gone to work in the sugar beet factory that looks out over the Wash. He worked there for the next forty years, but as a boy he would go down below with his father most Saturdays, and he invited me along so that I could take my birds in a basket to toss them over the water. It was a marvellous sight out by the sandbanks, with seals by the hundred lounging on them and my birds flying off to the horizon beyond which lies Lynn, but after my first experience I wonder I ever went again.

The first time I went the boat was headed for the prawning grounds way out in the Wash, so it took half a day to get there. Down below there was a fire going with seats all around it where the men sat and talked. A saucepan was put over the fire and tea, sugar and milk were all boiled up together in it. We drank out of jam jars. By being confined down there I got the smell of the fire in my stomach and I was sick for hours. I went up on deck and lay down at the front of the boat; I wouldn't have cared if I had died. Then Tubby's father put a piece of pork on a string and hung it over my face so it swayed with the sea. He kept saying, 'This is what you want, boy,' and I kept being sick. We were on the water all day, but by the end of it I'd stopped being sick and I'd never felt better in my life. When we came up to Lynn the men were cooking prawns down below, and they were beautiful.

One of the lads I was apprentice with at the time was the son of Mr Palmer, the second engineer on one of two boats, the *Fairy* and the *Sea Nymph*, that traded in grain all up the east coast as far as Leith in Scotland. So I asked Mr Palmer if he would take my birds with him and toss them when he was far out at sea. Then the birds had no choice but to keep going for mile after mile across the water home again. Mr Palmer would let those birds off anywhere: he had no sense of the right time to let them off, and short of a gale blowing he was as heedless of the weather as the barnacles on the bottom of his boat – but I hardly ever lost a pigeon. I would have to take the birds down to the boat just before casting-off time, even if it was the middle of the night, otherwise the rats would run up the ropes that tied the ship to the capstans on the dockside and kill them.

After five years as an apprentice I was earning £1 a week and was considered skilled enough by then to move on to an hourly rate for the two years' 'improving' that was standard in the trade before a man could call himself a member. Keeping pigeons for my own enjoyment took up any spare coppers I might have, but now I had the odd shilling in my pocket to buy some more birds. I had some luck here when a lot of miners and shipyard workers came down to Lynn from Wales and Newcastle to build the pumping station. The Depression had hit them hard. Being a sportsman and a lifelong football fanatic, I got on well with these blokes – and some of the men from Ashington, where the footballing Charlton brothers come from, turned out to be pigeon men. They had left their pigeons at home along with their families, because there was no work to be had there.

I don't know how they stayed so cheerful, but they were glad to be working in Lynn, then when the time came they were glad to be going home again. They had that ability to make the best of things when another chap would be worried sick, and I was told I had to go and stay with them to meet the pigeons. Scotland's Blue Devils were playing England in Glasgow that year and I had already set my heart on going. Nothing was easier in those days than taking detours on the railway. My mining friends lived just outside Ashington in a little village called North Seaton, a marvellous place on the side of a valley with the sea so close you could hear it. It was wild up there compared to Norfolk – great cliffs falling into the sea and rocks jutting out of it. There were some very good flyers in the village and in Ashington, and the stories they told of their birds had me in a trance. That's what finally set me up in racing, coming away from North Seaton with their stories in my ears and several first-rate stock birds they were so generous they had to give me. Nothing could stop me after that. I spent the money I'd put by on a racing clock.

The Lynn Flying Club met regularly in the stable yard of the Swan pub on what used to be the outskirts of Lynn, where the Wootton Road and the Gayton Road meet at the clock tower and turn in towards the centre of the town. There were formalities to be gone through. My loft had to be put on to the map of the pigeon-racing world. For each club it's a big world because pigeons race five hundred, maybe seven hundred miles every week at the height of the season – one week from Thurso in the very north of Scotland, the next from France or Spain. The distance from each race point to each loft has to be calculated precisely, not to the mile but to the yard: officials from the club visit the loft carrying a huge map, on a scale of six inches to one mile of ground, that shows clearly each house and its garden. Where exactly the loft is in the garden has to be paced out, then one of the officials brings out a pin and sticks it just there in the map, which is turned over so a circle can be drawn around the pinhole and the flyer's name attached. The margin of error of the pinprick can be guaranteed at ten yards or less, ten yards being about the diameter of a pinprick on a six-inch map.

Before computers took over the whole subject of mathematics the map was sent to a registered Official Calculator, usually a surveyor appointed by the Union, who would then carefully figure out the loft's longitude and latitude. Once he knew that, he turned to the system used in long-range artillery fire, the Great Circle system, which is the curve on old Mercator's chart, to plot the shortest distance around the earth from a race point, say Berwick, for which he also had the co-ordinates, to the loft. He would go through this process for each of the race points used by the club, so a flyer knew to the yard how far his birds had to fly when he sent them off on a race. If and when the birds got back home and their rings were in the clock it was possible, even before computers were used, to measure the average speed they had flown in yards per minute. What the flyer wants to know is the bird's velocity measured in yards per minute, then he'll know if it's won.

The most famous member of the Lynn club was a man we hardly ever saw, although he was always winning races. He never brought his own birds to marking-up night, nor did he deliver his clock to the Swan yard once the race was over and it was time for the officials to calculate velocities. There was nothing mysterious about him, though – he was the King, and he sent his lofts manager, Mr Jones. Mr Jones was a very old man when I first came to the club and I hardly caught sight of him before he retired. The man who took his place had been one of his pupils at the school in West Newton, where he had learnt enough about pigeons to be accepted in the Carrier Pigeon Service during the First World War. He'd had to pass a strict examination to prove his capabilities as fancier and trainer before he could enlist. Mr Jones had been only too glad to help him, and at the outbreak of war the royal birds were immediately volunteered for active service. This man was the natural choice as successor to Mr Jones because he lived on the estate at Sandringham – he was my predecessor, Ernest Steele.

5

The Royal Pigeon Fanciers

While the royal pigeons were at West Newton, in Steele's time, the Queen could stroll out from Sandringham to see them whenever she chose. Once I'd taken over from him, and the lofts I'd built at the end of my garden became the Royal Lofts, six miles of country road separated the Queen from her birds. I had no idea how close my new task would bring me to the Queen herself.

I dealt with Major Fellowes, the agent, and as a rule I dealt with him through his clerk, Mr Pillar. We seemed to get along all right in that first interview, when the job was offered to me. I was taken home from York Cottage in the same black car by the estate's driver, Jack Benstead. It was a terribly cold winter that year, and the snow froze on the ground right from Boxing Day to late April. There were drifts up either side of the road, and across the big fields where farmers had dug out the hedgerows hurdles had been put out to stop the snow piling up into mountains. A lot more hedgerows have disappeared over the years since then, so that more fields have to be set out with hurdles come wintertime.

If I did not entertain any notion of meeting the Queen, the thought crossed my mind that the Queen Mother might learn of my appointment, if I accepted it, because I had already met her several times at the big Sandringham Flower Show which she always attends. She was Queen Elizabeth the first time I met her and she was there with King George VI. A regular feature of the afternoon was a cricket match, the Sandringham XI against another local side, and that year I was umpire for the West Norfolk XI. After the match all the cricket people were introduced to the King and Queen. I was so dumbfounded by how beautiful she was that I hardly noticed the King. When I went home I told Gladys, 'I've never seen a more perfect piece of flesh.'

As well as the cricket match there was a Fur and Feathers Show every year. I kept a dozen or so show birds both before and after I took on the royal birds, and I would enter a few. They did look good – not a bent feather, and all the colourings bright as can be. They were fed the best food, rape seed and peanut-crush rich in oils to get their feathers like silk, and they were bred purely for the sake of their graceful appearance. Beyond exercising, as I do with all the birds, they lived the life of Riley except for the few days a year when I would show them, after the season was over in the autumn, and at the Sandringham Fur and Feathers Show in the summer. I would train them to pose on an inverted flowerpot in the show-cage, their tails pointing straight at the floor, chests out, wings folded low down so their line was perfect. By trailing a small stick around the cage I would teach them to walk in a circle as neat as a roundabout, and any visitors to my lofts who knew what they were about, like Steele, I would invite to handle them, to get the birds quite happy in a stranger's hands. Only the judges handled them at the show, and never the Queen Mother, but she was at the prizegivings and she remembered me.

Sitting in the car next to Jack Benstead that first time I was brought home from York Cottage, however, I was having my doubts as to the wisdom of taking on the job of Royal Lofts manager, no matter how exciting the prospect was. I mulled over the last part of the interview, when Major Fellowes had turned to Mr Pillar and asked, 'What did we pay old Steele?'

Mr Pillar told him that thirty bob a week had been taken as

the value of the job. Perhaps they thought it was generous to offer me thirty bob a week for looking after the pigeons, because for that Steele had also done the gardening. But as soon as I got home I rang Mr Pillar, whom I found a delightful man, to tell him I couldn't accept that wage.

'Just a minute, Mr Rush,' said Mr Pillar, and the line went silent.

In less than a minute he was back on the phone, having rung through to Major Fellowes. I was to have £2 a week. So everything was settled, and the Queen had only to accept me formally. I would receive a telephone call, Mr Pillar told me, when arrangements would be made for Jack Benstead to drive aong the icy roads again to take me to York Cottage to see Major Fellowes.

Gladys was home when I got back, but I rang Mr Pillar before I told her what was up. I didn't want Major Fellowes going to the Queen if I only had to change my mind afterwards, which would have been churlish.

'You'll never guess what that was about', I said to Gladys when I put the phone down.

She was very pleased for me. When I'd told her the news we had a little celebration in our back room on our own, since it was too soon to tell anyone.

The very next day Jack Benstead came for me, and Major Fellowes's handshake was like getting the royal seal of approval. I went straight to the Royal Lofts, and to my surprise Major Fellowes came with me. The Queen was at the big house with her family – I could see the flag flying – but there was no one in the park as we went through to the back gate and around to West Newton. The school was deserted, too, with hardly a footprint in the snow around it, but a path had been cleared to Mr Jones's old house and the lofts.

It was a while since I had been there, and I could tell at a glance there was a deal of sorting out to do. The lofts were a good size but there were maybe three hundred birds filling up the perches, all their feathers fluffed out against the cold so that they looked even more crowded than they were.

'Fine birds, I understand, Rush,' said the Major.

'They were when Steele was on his feet,' I said, 'So they must be now, those that are meant to be here,' and I reached out to pick up a mealy that was sitting comfortably on a lower perch. A mealy is a greyish-silver bird with one or two red stripes on its wings, as a rule the offspring of a light blue bird with a red chequered bird, and very attractive it can be. But I was suspicious of this bird – the look of it wasn't the look of the royal stock or the look of Steele's type of pigeon.

It was easy enough to tell. The royal birds all had the cipher EIIR included in the number on their rings, or if they were old enough they would have GVI engraved on the ring, and the mealy I picked up had neither. It was someone else's bird, a stray that had come in on the races for feed, found the accommodation to its taste, and not left again. When I got down to it I found more than fifty strays amongst the royal birds – all on to a good thing, as they thought.

Not any more. I didn't want any Tom, Dick or Harry's blood mixing with that of the Queen's birds. I separated all of them out and took down their numbers, so that I could find out whose they were through the Royal Pigeon Racing Association in Cheltenham and set about repatriating them to their rightful lofts. Every pigeon's number is logged on a computer, and if anyone finds a stray racer that won't continue its homeward journey after a rest and a drink, or one that has died, the RPRA should be contacted. The owner will always be grateful for news, however sad.

Having eliminated all the intruders in the Royal Lofts, I could agree with Major Fellowes that they were fine birds. It would be a problem choosing the few I would take with me to start the new lofts – so many of them were beauties, looking me straight in the eye as if to say: 'Dispose of me if you dare!'

You talk to pigeons with your hands, as well as by looking

them in the eye and lavishing them with soothing noises to bring out their best. Pick up a bird right and it will enjoy the feel of your hand. You show it one hand and take it up with the other by bringing your open hand down on its back, then the thumb of that hand gently holds the wings while the bird's legs slip between your first and second fingers and its body is cupped nicely in your palm. It will relax, and there aren't many occasions other than egg sitting when a bird indulges in relaxation. If it's awake it will often as not be craning its neck around like a nosey parker or strutting on its perch, a show-off and a fidget, as if it can never for a moment take being at home in its loft for granted. But if you hold the bird so that your hands give it a sense of security it will sit there quietly, a picture of calm and comfort. Then your hands can tell you more about the bird than you will ever find out by looking at it. A fit bird feels like nothing so much as solid india rubber all through because its muscles are so well tuned and developed – the racing pigeon is perhaps the most muscular animal in the world. Its flight muscles alone, the greater pectorals, make up one third of its total weight when it's properly trained. They bulge on either side of its keel, like a weight-lifter's might; but amazingly, for all its solid muscle, the bird feels incredibly light in your hands – 'corky', we call it.

You can tell a bird's character by the way it feels in your hand, and character has as much to do with winning races as do fitness and good breeding – only it's more difficult to describe. When you cup the bird in both your hands, its firm and feathered roundness makes you tingle. You can feel the energy ready to propel the bird through the air for hundreds and hundreds of miles. Its heart beats much faster than a man's, its body temperature is a good ten degress higher, it's warm and quick and vibrant by nature – and the mystery is that it should know so much without being told. When he holds the bird, the fancier shares a tiny, tiny part of this mystery, sensing the creature's individuality.

So I picked up and talked to and handled all the two hundred-odd birds in the Royal Lofts, and I marvelled at their pedigrees, which I discovered from Steele's loft books and Mr Jones's loft books before him. Some of their pedigrees went all the way back to the first royal birds, which were the gift of King Leopold of the Belgians to the Prince of Wales (later Edward VII) just over one hundred years ago in 1886. Belgium is the true home of racing pigeons. The Belgians have been at it longer and in greater numbers than anyone else in the world, and King Leopold II had been a strong fancier. When the Prince of Wales admired his birds on a visit to Belgium, straightaway he picked out some of his best and sent them across the Channel.

There had been pigeon societies in England since the middle of the eighteenth century, all of them meeting at pubs like so many do still today, such as the Columbarian Society at the Globe in Fleet Street, and the Feather Club at the Griffin. But while British fanciers were still breeding birds for show – or to be shot by the hundred at so-called sporting occasions – the Belgians were regularly racing birds over distance. This is even more remarkable than it sounds, because in England and most other countries the sport of racing pigeons had to wait for the construction of the railway network before it could get off the ground, so to speak. In Belgium they were so keen that they found other means of transporting the birds a hundred or more miles to race each other home again, and by 1840 fanciers there had bred the Belgian homer, the modern racing bird. This combined the good qualities of a whole range of former breeds and knocked any other racing bird out of the competition. The homer is superior in endurance, intelligence, speed and size because all the breeds that went into its making had these qualities and the homer has inherited them at perhaps their ultimate best. Eastern Carrier, Camus, Horseman, Dragoon, Cumulet, Tumbler, Beard and Smerle – the Belgians took from all of them and produced the homer we know today.

Some of the very first homers in Britain, where Dragoons, Smerles, Owls and Flying Tumblers were already racing each other, were those in the new lofts at Sandringham, the gift of King Leopold.

Seven years passed. The Prince of Wales was busy elsewhere, no doubt. The birds waited, untrained, prisoners in an aviary like common or garden parrots, the secret of their homing instinct and their marvellous breeding hidden away, so much treasure waiting to be discovered. Then the Prince's son, the Duke of York, who would one day be King George V, grew curious. The sport was becoming popular in Britain, so popular that a Federation of clubs was set up in Lancashire in 1890. They could fly distance on the South Road without crossing to the Continent, which made it easier for them and for their birds, but there were soon to be Federations covering the whole of the country. Not only had the railways made it possible to take the birds in large numbers to distant race points, but railwaymen had taken to fancying in droves. They were to be the aristocrats of the sport for years and years. Now it was to become the sport of kings, as well. A racing loft was set up for the Duke of York in 1893 with some of the birds from Belgium and their offspring.

At this the Prince of Wales sat up and took notice. He ordered another racing loft to be kitted out for himself, and training began. Teams of pigeons swirled through the air above Sandringham, the Duke's birds and the Prince's birds eyeing each other with interest, returning to their own lofts with that pigeon-brained certainty that no other loft would do, no matter how close or well-connected. I wonder, did the men charged with training them discuss their respective prospects, or was the rivalry too deadly serious for the usual congenialities that pigeon folk are famous for? Without a doubt competition was fierce, because just six years later the royal birds started to make their mark. In 1899 the Duke's birds won third and fifth place in the national race from Lerwick in the Shetland Isles. He should have been pleased, and perhaps he was, but his father, the Prince, was even more pleased; one of his birds won first place. They must have spurred each other on, those competing royal birds, over 515 miles, to be that close.

The young Duke was the true fancier. Till the end of his life he knew all his birds, all their numbers and pedigrees. He spent as much time as he possibly could with the birds, and one day when he got to his lofts he found a stranger there, a knowledgeable stranger. It was Mr Jones, who had been village schoolmaster at West Newton since 1881 and a fancier since boyhood, and that day the friendship began that was to last their whole lives. The Duke persuaded his father to merge the royal birds under Mr Jones's expert care. The Prince became King in 1901 and the Duke moved up a notch to become Prince of Wales himself. Then in 1910 he was crowned King George V and that was when he built the house next to the school for Mr Jones, and next to the house the Royal Lofts which my mate Steele would one day tend, when Mr Jones had to give up, long after he retired as a schoolmaster in 1922.

There would be a grand sale of royal birds once I had chosen the few I would take with me to start the new Royal Lofts. I wanted birds good for breeding, not racing, since they would have to be prisoners in their new quarters. I wanted good foster parents so that the breeders could rear their first batch properly but provide more young to stock the loft – the foster parents would be old birds, highly experienced in the art of rearing young. I wanted all their pedigrees to include notable long-distance winners, because all racers are looking for birds that can bring home classic trophies. And I wanted the original Delmotte-Jurion blood of the very first royal birds to carry on flying the royal colours from Gaywood. After much consideration, I took thirty-six birds and their nest boxes to Gaywood in an estate lorry. My own birds I had already sold off or given away – not without a few tears and fond kisses of farewell. For the royal birds to get some fresh air and sunshine whenever they could I built an aviary beside my lofts – not the grand affair they were used to, just a plain wire mesh enclosure such as you might expect to find beside the lofts of an ordinary bloke.

My lofts are at the end of the garden, positioned so that the doors face the back windows. That way the lofts face leeward; the birds prefer to land up-wind. There is grass in front of the lofts for the young birds to hop out on to when they're learning to fly, and where they can all bathe in the galvanised-iron pan I set out for them in good weather. The most vital matter with pigeons is keeping clean, preening and bathing, and the big priority is keeping the air they breathe in the loft as fresh as the air outside it. The direct ancestor of the racing pigeon was the rock dove that lived and nested all year round on exposed rock ledges above the sea. Pigeons cannot thrive in a loft that traps the air inside it, because the birds start breathing the ammonia of their droppings and the obnoxious gases they've already exhaled. There's nothing worse than hearing a pigeon wheezing because it has respiratory disease, which it will contract in a closed loft. To keep the air circulating and the damp – as well as vermin – out, lofts are always built on posts so that they stand a good foot and a half off the ground, as mine do.

Wood is the best material for building a loft, unless you have as much money as it takes to build a good one with brick or stone, like the Queen Mother's friend Mr C.J. Williams, who is a breeder of marvellous birds. But I work with wood and I like it. Wood doesn't harbour damp, and it's not cold to the touch like brick or concrete. True, it's hot in summer and cold in winter, but the whole length of the loft is open dowelling from the waist up so it's never stifling, even in a heatwave; and if it's cold the birds' feathers are a wonderful means of keeping a body snug – or at least keeping it at a safe temperature, even in a severe winter.

The fancier's own comfort has to be considered in building a loft. The difference between a wild and a tame pigeon, let alone a winner and a straggler, is the amount of time a man spends with his birds. If a man is uncomfortable – if he has to squeeze through a narrow door to get into the loft, then stoop with his head jammed against a low roof – he won't be inclined to visit often and linger chatting with his feathered friends. So there are big double sliding doors into my lofts, and height enough inside for me to stand easy with my cap on – perhaps with a bird perched on my head. Standing in the loft, a fancier will probably find himself a perch for several birds at once, one sitting on his shoe, one happily looking at the world from his shoulder, another tickling his ear. It would be a pity to have to shake them all off because the bird the fancier wants to pick up is out of reach – to have a big open space in a loft is nothing but a hindrance. It is partly for that reason that lofts are compartmentalised, so that wherever the fancier stands he can reach out and pick up the bird he wants. Compartments are also needed to separate young birds from old ones, hens from cocks during the winter months, and stock birds from racing teams.

I had thoroughly disinfected the lofts once my own birds were gone from them, and before the royal birds arrived in the lorry from Sandringham I had distempered the walls to make them bright, white, clean and cheerful. They had served me well when I was racing in my own name. Those lofts I built at Highbury are good and sturdy – they've stood for fifty years now – and in due course I was by no means ashamed to take the Queen into them.

6

The Queen Visits Highbury

teele and his wife were tickled pink that his scheme for me had succeeded and I was to take his place.

'Don't suppose you were offered Mr Jones's house, Len?' he said. 'Well, I never had the chance of that house, either.'

It was a standing joke about the house, because Steele lived in somewhat primitive conditions where he was – not that he wasn't happy enough to be there. The grounds of Sandringham House are marvellous. The old cottage where Steele had been brought up, with its huge fireplace and great oak beams showing through the ceiling, had gone to his sister when old Mr Steele died. When Steele was a boy there had been trophies and cups all around the room that his father had won for his Sandringham pigs – old Mr Steele had been famous all over Norfolk as a pig man.

When he was young Steele had the most terrible stutter, and couldn't say his own name to save his life. One day Queen Mary, King George V's consort, came up to him in the garden and asked him a question – to which he could make no reply whatever, being stuck till his eyes bulged on the first letter of what he wanted to say. The next thing anyone knew, Steele wasn't at home. Queen Mary had sent him to London for his stutter to be cured by a speech therapist. He had made great friends with the Queen after that. Steele and his wife had one daughter and Queen Mary had one, Princess Mary, and the two little girls would play together whenever the royal family was at Sandringham. The Queen would just knock on the door of Steele's house and walk in, as if it was another home to her.

Steele had been a great source of help and advice to me on my birds ever since I was a young man. He'd handled generations of my birds and been like a godfather to them, bringing out their best. Steele died just a couple of months after the Queen first visited my house, but I was glad that he died knowing his beloved royal pigeons were in caring hands.

One thing I had in common with Steele as Royal Lofts manager was the luck to be married to a woman who had some feeling for the birds. Steele had first met his wife at the school in West Newton where she also went as a small child. They had often been set to write out the pedigrees of the royal birds for Mr Jones, so they were aware of the traditions long before Steele took over. Right up to the time when Steele became ill and she had to look after him Mrs Steele would help out with the birds. If you look at the membership rolls of pigeon clubs across the country most fanciers are men, or so it would seem. But more and more these days are signing in 'Mr and Mrs Whatever-the-name-is', because it's hard for a man to be a successful flyer if his wife isn't just about as keen as he is, or at least keen for him to do well with his birds.

When I was away from home at football matches Gladys would look after the birds as well as ever I did. There were birds she took a fancy to, and not for the reasons I might fancy a bird – but then there aren't always *reasons* for what you do fancy, like the bloom on its feathers or the firmness of its greater pectorals. There's whatever strikes you as a God-given uniqueness in a bird, or it might be that the bird seems marvellously typical of its strain, a chip off the old block. You're always looking for that special bird that will have the head and the heart to keep flying all the hours of daylight no matter what, the bird that puts getting home to the loft above the need for water, corn or sleep. You train the bird and care for it to get it fit, and you try to breed the right physique for the job, which involves the general principles, so to speak, of what you fancy. Then it's down to the individual bird – its special quality – and it might be something you can't for the life of you put a name to. Of a Saturday afternoon, then, it would be Gladys as often as not who timed in the birds returning from a race. Sometimes this got her down. 'I wasted all afternoon looking for pigeons, Len,' she would say – but not if one of them had got home in good time and there was a chance it had won a race.

Not long after the royal birds came to live with Gladys and me, I had an invitation to go to Norwich to talk on the wireless about being Royal Lofts manager. Gladys came with me on the train, and the chap doing the interview was so polite it was easy for both of us to talk into a microphone about how delighted we were to be associated with Her Majesty through the royal birds.

A day or two later, Major Fellowes and Mr Pillar came to visit. Now I don't live in a mansion, and when they came they had rather a shock – I could see it on their faces. The agent at Sandringham does live in a mansion, and Mr Pillar was obviously not short of a bob or two. But when they came into our back parlour and looked through the window at the new Royal Lofts at the end of the garden, beyond the washing that was frozen stiff on the line, there was a silence.

I told them all thirty-six royal birds were fighting fit and luxuriating in the spaciousness of their new home after the crowding at West Newton. The cocks and the hens were still separated because the time for mating was still a month away. Because they're so fit and well fed and housed, racing pigeons will happily mate the whole year through, although possibly that particularly bitter winter might have deterred them.

The Major was worried that the entire royal stock would be wiped out by Jack Frost.

'Norfolk is good for pigeons,' I told him. 'We can be terrible cold in Norfolk, but it's one of the best and driest places in the country. What the birds hate most is the damp. They can take the cold – they can even take a cold wind better than they can take the damp. Not an east wind – that would kill a bird like it would kill a man if it kept blowing into a loft in winter, so a loft built facing east needs shutters against a bitter night. But a loft built facing a wet wind, a south-wester, that would never do. All manner of parasites breed in the damp and you'll have birds sick with gut worms and canker, and then you'll have one generation after another riddled with parasites, diarrhoea, tuberculosis and feather rot. Those birds down there,' I said, pointing out of the window to the lofts, 'they're cold, I'll grant you. But they don't mind, and I'd be a fool to mind for them. If I coddle them and keep 'em warm, the Queen would never race another winner.'

'No, that would never do,' the Major agreed. Gladys brought us coffee and cakes and we were all basking in the warmth of the fire, quite happy that the birds were getting on all right without the benefit of such home comforts. 'The reason we came here, Rush,' said the Major at last, 'was to congratulate you. In your speech on the radio you spoke very well of old Steele, and you showed great loyalty by your remarks about the Queen. I'd like you to accept another pound a week.'

That was all right by me. I could tell we were getting on very well indeed. But what he said next gave Gladys and me a real shock.

'We must have the Queen come here,' he said.

The Queen come to Highbury? We called the house Highbury because I supported Arsenal then as I do now, and Gladys was nearly as keen on football as I was. But Highbury is a plain man's semi-detached home, and an Englishman's home may be his castle in a manner of speaking, but the Queen was accustomed to the real thing. I looked around me and the walls seemed very close and in need of fresh wallpaper. I couldn't imagine the Queen sitting on our leatherette sofa, which was covered in little cracks because it was twenty-seven years old, like the rest of the furniture, and the chenille tablecloth wasn't much younger. But Gladys was smiling.

'That would be a great honour for us,' she said. 'Wouldn't it, Len?'

The Queen's first visit to our house was arranged in no time at all. The bitter weather continued and our pipes kept freezing, and I developed a terrible cold. But the birds were fit, I told myself, and that was all that mattered – the Queen would see a tidy loft and healthy birds. She would come on the following Sunday at twelve-thirty, we were told, with Prince Philip and a lady-in-waiting. Gladys and I were under strict instructions not to say anything about it to anyone. The Queen's security was at stake, of course. But we were nervous, and it was difficult to think about anything else.

There was a very rich man who went to our local chapel. He was very religious and one of the owners of the Peterborough brickworks. I would have staked my life on his honesty. When I knew that the Queen was coming, in spite of being told not to say anything I decided to tell this man in all confidence. He was a great friend and a very responsible person, as I thought.

Just before half past twelve on the big day Gladys and I were dressed and tidy, the house was as clean as a new pin, the birds had fresh wood shavings on the floor and we were all tensely waiting. I looked out of the front window to see if the royal car was coming up the road yet – and saw the owner of the Peterborough brickworks, his wife and half Gaywood chapel gathered outside on the pavement. He'd told them all.

I had betrayed a trust and the evidence was there on the pavement for everyone to see – for the Queen to see. The thought flashed through my mind that perhaps I had committed treason. I felt doomed, as cold as the snow outside the window, at the thought of what would happen next. At any second the Queen's motor would be turning into Kent Road and the Queen or Prince Philip would doubtless tell the driver to keep going, not to stop at our house. There would be displeasure, the sack, the rest of my life to regret it in. . . . The ringing of the telephone was like a sword falling on my head.

'Mr Rush? It was a lady's voice. It was the Queen's lady-in-waiting, Lady Mary Morison. 'Would you mind very much if the Queen didn't come today?' she asked. 'The roads are impassable here with the snow. If it is convenient to you' – convenient to *me*? – 'she will come tomorrow instead.'

I never told them. I left them standing outside in the snow, and as far as I'm concerned they're standing there now. I never afterwards said a word to my friend about it, and no more did he mention it to me. He was a gentleman, which goes to show that even gentlemen aren't always honest. It was a hard lesson, and my appointment as Royal Lofts manager was very nearly too brief to reflect any glory.

Having been in such a panic and at such a pitch of nerves might account for how calm both Gladys and I were the next day. Gladys went through the whole business of cleaning and polishing and tidying and dusting the ornaments she'd been through the morning before, and there I was in the lofts with fresh wood shavings, sweeping out what I'd put down only yesterday. I looked out of the front window more than once, holding my breath, but the pavement was bare. Not a soul stood waiting. Then a big black car came quietly up the empty street. Just an ordinary car, no flag on the bonnet, no crest above the windscreen, but I knew this was it. I went outside to meet the Queen.

When the car pulled up in front of Highbury the chauffeur hopped out quick as a flash to open the back door. He leaned in and pulled out a plaid rug that had been covering the Queen's knees. This he threw over his arm and offered his other hand to Her Majesty. I noticed how gracefully she got out of the car, then she was walking straight towards me with her hand extended, smiling all over her face. I tried to be gentle with her hand, and I hoped I was doing the right thing by bowing over it, but she was so natural, right from the first moment of meeting her. And because the Queen's face, and everything about her, was so familiar to me – as to every one of her subjects – from when she was a little girl, when the time came there didn't seem anything in the least strange about welcoming her to my home.

'This is a great honour, Your Majesty,' I said.

Such lovely eyes she has. Lady Mary Morison was directly behind her, and Prince Philip strolled up to us, looking all around him.

As we shook hands he said, 'I see you're a builder, Mr Rush.'

There was some wood stacked up by the garage with a small pile of snow on top of it, waiting for the snow to melt before it could be used in an outside job I had going. It stood there for months that winter. I led them the short distance past the wood, up the front path to the front door, where I stood aside for Her Majesty to enter.

'After you, Mr Rush,' she said.

There was a huddle of us in the hallway by the stairs as I introduced Gladys. She had practised curtseying with her sister Flossie – Gladys had told Flossie the Queen was coming because she saw her every day and it was unthinkable not to tell her, just as it was unthinkable that Flossie would not keep the secret. But Flossie was a large, tall, awkward woman and Gladys didn't curtsey to the Queen anything like she'd done it when practising, when Flossie had just about held her upright. But it was a neat little bob she did, and soon we were gathered comfortably in the front room.

The Queen admired our open fire and as she warmed her hands told us how much she enjoyed the wood fires they always had at Balmoral and Sandringham. At the Palace and at Windsor, she said, they could only have central heating.

On this, the first of many visits to the Royal Lofts, I was to discover that the Queen would give you all of her attention, and one of the things that makes her special is that, having met such a tremendous number of people in her life – perhaps more people than anyone has ever met in the history of the world – she knows very well who *you* are. You sense this from the start, her knowledge of human nature. There's no mistaking her intelligence. Instead of this being unnerving, it does away with airs and graces and leaves a body with no choice but to be himself. I always let the Queen speak first, but she was unfailingly generous, so that responding to her was just like falling off a log.

Prince Philip only came with the Queen on that first visit. After that he left the Queen to her birds because they are a special interest of hers. Prince Philip is certainly a sportsman, but he prefers horses and shooting and he would pull the Queen's leg about her pigeons. He remarked wryly on that first visit that they hadn't won much lately, but when he turned to the Queen to get her confirmation of this she told him she was sure they were about to have a new lease of life.

So we went into the back parlour to look over the garden to the new Royal Lofts, and we started talking pigeons, the Queen and I. She was delighted to hear how well I thought of her birds. I think she was pleased that they were in a regular loft at the end of a fancier's garden and she was eager to see them.

'Just three dozen birds,' she said, 'the first generation of a new loft.' So few birds, she told me, meant that she wouldn't be confused as to which one was which. She said she had always been overwhelmed at the idea of knowing all the birds because there were so many in the lofts. She was amazed that Mr Jones and Mr Steele could recognise each bird at a glance. But, she thought, she could start getting to know them afresh, and perhaps even keep track of them when the lofts were returned to full strength.

Then I went with the Queen and Prince Philip down the garden path, which I had gritted for safety's sake, past the rockery and the patch of snow where the potatoes would be planted, to the lofts, leaving Lady Mary Morison with Gladys by the fire.

The aviary took up some space on the grass in front of the lofts, but there was no green to be seen anyway, the sky was overcast, and the whole landscape was buried in old snow. Shades of grey took the colour right out of the paint on the outside of the lofts to leave them dun-coloured in a drab world. There were no birds in the aviary: there was no pleasure for them in sitting outside on a dank and freezing day. The lofts looked strangely empty with just thirty-six birds in them, the hens in one compartment and the cocks in another. Telling the sexes apart isn't difficult if you know what to look for, but the bird's plumage gives no clue, and it's not a question of upending a bird and looking hard at its rump. Both sexes look alike from that angle, except when the hen is about to lay an egg. Then the vent bones on either side of its cloaca start to pull apart to allow the egg to be laid – the hen is eggy, we flyers say. By the time a bird is eggy, it's been mated, and you are in no doubt about its sex. Before that, the surest way to tell a hen is to look for old-fashioned feminine virtues in the bird: if a bird is demure, delicately moulded, with an elegant head and neck and a gentle voice, it's a hen. On the other hand if a bird is pushy and pompous, bold of eye, noisy, with a big head and a big wattle, it's a cock. After a while a fancier makes as few mistakes with telling the sex of a pigeon as he does with telling the sex of a person – perhaps fewer mistakes nowadays, with earrings and trousers on both lots of humans.

I took the Queen and Prince Philip first into the cocks' compartment. They were spread about the perches, their feather-jackets puffed right out for insulation, and they were quiet because of the season, being celibate and cold. There was nothing cocky about them at all.

'They're not suffering so much as they appear to be, Your

Majesty,' I told the Queen. They looked as miserable as refugees from a hot country.

Prince Philip asked if they were missing all the other birds, because he believed them to be gregarious by nature.

'No,' I told him. 'They're not like the old passenger pigeons that lived in great hordes, then gradually became extinct because their numbers were so heavily reduced by farmers with guns. Racing pigeons don't like to live crowded together. They'd much rather have more space than they need, than less.'

It was much more pleasant inside the loft than outside it, despite the open sides, and the three of us got down to looking at the birds individually. Noticing that I called each bird by its number, the Queen wanted to know if I named the pigeons, and asked if it wouldn't be easier to identify them if they had names.

'No, Your Majesty,' I said. 'The only birds I've ever had that I called by name were my first two birds, Baldwin and Bad Luck. No one could have had better luck than being given the bird named Bad Luck for his very first stock – he was a King's Cup winner, and I bred another King's Cup winner from him. Such a daft name for a bird like that! Perhaps that's why I've never named them. My Uncle Herbert, who was a shepherd, knew every one of his sheep, but you wouldn't expect him to name them.'

Her Majesty said she was sure I had always known each and every individual bird in my lofts, but thought that remembering lots of numbers would be more like thinking in code.

'I can always refer to the loft books should I need to,' I said, 'using the ring number to find out the number I've given it, but I can't say I've ever had to do that. Now, it's true that in any good loft there's many birds alike because a fancier is always breeding to type. He's trying to perfect his own type, to produce his own strain from the original stock – Delmotte-Jurion, say, like most of the royal blood here. He'll want to breed out all the qualities he doesn't like – a deep keel, or a tail sticking out. I don't like to see a pigeon's tail sticking out. But there's always something about each bird in my loft that I do like – the shape it makes, the cast of its eye, the tail touching the floor. There's no mistaking which bird is which, and when they breed the young birds will have numbers, and the numbers of their parents will be forever associated with the young birds' numbers – I do believe I would find names a sight more confusing.'

The birds had grown tame over the last few weeks and they were happy enough to be handled and shown off to the Queen, their benefactor and provider. Prince Philip had a go at handling one and I was pleased the bird didn't take exception to being in a stranger's hands. It liked the warmth, and the Prince smiled at it.

'These are fine lofts, Mr Rush,' he said. He asked me if I had built them myself, which I confirmed.

Since I had chosen the birds as breeding stock they were all pigeons that had proved themselves both in the basket – that is, racing – and as producers of fine young. Some were sedate old grandparents I had chosen for their huge experience of rearing youngsters. These I would use as foster parents to the second batches of eggs which the more important breeders would lay, once the first-reared youngsters were strong enough to jump out of the nest bowl and chase their parents for food.

Good foster parents are important in a loft. Sometimes you get a bird that is very, very good at producing pigeon milk, which is the thick curd secreted in the crop of both male and female pigeons while they sit on the eggs, anticipating the hatching of the young. When squabs hatch they gobble it down and within two days they've doubled in weight, reaching into their parents' beaks and bloating themselves with it. It's as thick as the first milking of a cow, known as the beestings, which I like as much as the squabs seem to like their pigeon milk – beestings make a really beautiful solid custard. Some birds will go on producing the milk longer than others and they make the finest foster parents, giving the youngsters the best possible start in life. It was this sort of detail noted in Steele's loft books that had helped me decide which birds would come to Highbury to continue in the royal service as foster parents. Meanwhile the real parents would sit on pot eggs until they got bored with waiting for them to hatch; then they would produce another round to stock the Royal Lofts.

As a rule it's the birds you want to race that you keep from rearing another round of young, since it's tiring work feeding a hungry squab, but I had no plans to race the royal birds I'd brought from Sandringham that year. You can retrain birds to a new loft once they have produced young there, and I would retrain the old birds once breeding was done. But there was too great a chance that they would head straight back to the West Newton lofts if I sent them away to Thurso or Banff on a race. So there would be no point in trying to race the first year, except in the young bird races later in the season. Then I would race the squabs that would be born in the new loft once they were several months old and ready and trained for racing.

I had just about decided on which hen to mate with which cock, which of course the Queen wanted to know. She understands all about the genetics of the business, but then she's a very clever lady. I told her she'd forgotten more than I'd ever know. I just knew the birds, more like a shepherd knows his sheep. With the qualities I saw in the birds it was possible to form some hopes about their potential for racing long distance when they were mature and their prospects for the coming season's young bird races. The Queen was so absorbed in the birds that she didn't seem to notice the cold.

'You'll mate them in the spring, I suppose?' she asked, and I told her I mated them on 14 February, which was romantic but also happened to be a good date for conceiving young racers. Their moult would be at the right stage for August and the first competitive events.

The Queen asked me what the birds were like when they first hatched, and to tell her something about moulting.

'They have clumps of downy yellow hair all over them when they're hatched,' I said. 'They're tremendously ugly, completely helpless. Blind, wobbly things, a sight for sore eyes. Then before you know it, the feathers start through the skin in tracts, each one in a little sheath, even the little coverlets of the head and body, and the sheaths open up like the bird is coming into bloom. So by the time it's four weeks old it even looks like a pigeon, only the feathers are dull – and by the time it's six weeks old, it's started to moult. But a good moult is a sign of good health, even though the poor bird looks terrible, nearly as bare as when it came out of the egg. Some of them look like they've been plucked, poor things – little scrawny neck showing, bald-headed. They're not raced when they're in that condition, or whenever the moult is heavy. I don't even train them until they're about ten weeks old, when they've lost their second primary flights – that's the second wing feather, counting from the inside. There are ten primary flight feathers, with number one the big one on the outside, so it's number nine I wait for them to shed before putting them in the basket.'

I showed the Queen and Prince Philip how the feathers were arranged on the wings and in what order they moulted – moulting is a very orderly affair, done once every year from top to toe, in such a manner that the bird is hardly ever badly incapacitated by lack of grown feathers.

When birds aren't in the peak of condition no man who cares about them sends them off racing, I told them, because he doesn't want to lose them.

Prince Philip asked if many birds were lost during races.

'As many as a million a year,' I said. 'Some fall in with gangs of street pigeons and take to scavenging – good riddance to them, if they should be so stupid, and the ones that take to the fields – but power cables and telephone wires claim a lot of lives, especially in bad weather when the birds fly low. Then there's fog, that's treacherous, and thunder and lightning – birds will be struck down or forced to land on water when they can't swim. Up north there are hawks terrorising the skies. And then there's the farmer with his shotgun. There are dozens of hazards for the pigeon flying home over hundreds of miles of uncharted land – more when there's water to cross. The sheer exhaustion of a race of five hundred or more miles makes me count it a miracle whenever one gets home, win or lose. And I'm sorry to say Your Majesty's birds have another problem. By and large fanciers are the best and most honest of people, but there are those who will be sorely tempted to keep a royal bird, to breed from it, should they find one resting on its way – there it is on the ring for everyone to see, EIIR, one of Your Majesty's birds. I shall lose more birds than most, like Steele did, because of that. But every fancier experiences losses. I sent a bird to Pau once, on the borders of Spain, seven hundred miles off. It got back, then I sent it again the next year – and it didn't get back. I've always regretted that. Remembering that bird still makes me downhearted. You know, Your Majesty, I think pigeon racing is cruel.'

At that the Queen gave me one of her beautiful smiles. 'But they're trained, Mr Rush,' was her reply.

It was time to return to the warmth of the house and see Gladys and Lady Mary Morison again. We went in through the breakfast room to sit in the lounge, where Gladys and Lady Mary had been getting along like a house on fire, I could tell.

'I notice you're keen on football, Mr Rush,' the Queen commented.

She said it with a touch of banter in her voice, and when I looked across at her I had to laugh, there was such a twinkle in her eye. Of course she had noticed how the walls of the breakfast room were hung all over with framed photographs of my favourite teams – the Arsenal in 1925 and the Lynn team that played Aston Villa in the English Cup in 1906 – with pride of place going to a huge signed picture of Stanley Matthews running full tilt at a ball. There's also a picture of Gladys and me looking rather solemn on our wedding day, but it's hard to see for the number of footballers all around it.

Major Fellowes had told her I had played in the King's Lynn team as a young man, the Queen added, perhaps to be sure I didn't think she was making fun of me in any way.

Over the next twenty-two years the Queen and I would talk about football whenever she visited her pigeons and me, as she did in all but four of those years, and it was marvellous to know that my greatest passion – even beyond my passion for the birds – was shared by her. One instance of her kindness and thoughtfulness came when I happened to mention to her on one visit that I hadn't been able to get tickets for Hampden Park that year, for the Scotland–England match. It would be the first one I had missed since 1933. A regular visitor to our house at that time was Major Blewitt, who was Assistant Keeper of the Privy Purse, and he called the very next day to let me know that the Queen was arranging for tickets to be sent.

7

My Two Great Loves: Part One

When I wasn't playing football as a young man I was watching it being played by the professionals all over the country. The best team I ever saw play was Scotland's Blue Devils when they thrashed England 5–0 in 1928, and if it wasn't just coincidence that that was the first game I ever took Gladys to then it was something else – like a good omen for Gladys and me – because it's not a romantic memory, I swear it. They were the best. That was the most exciting day of my eighteen years of life, being in London with my own girlfriend watching those Blue Devils – they were so brilliant they were uncanny, because all but one of the forward line were men of five foot five inches or less and they looked like boys running rings around full-grown men. Gladys and I cheered them for all we were worth. But football was a game her whole family was mad on. From the very beginning it was a subject we talked about endlessly. And the love of it was the one thing I had in common with Gladys's family, because her old man did not approve of me.

Gladys was one in a thousand. I don't think I was meant for her, but I know she was meant for me. I hadn't given her a second look when I first met her, and no more did she notice me. She and her sister Flossie were the daughters of a barber on the London Road and they were both in the choir of the Tower Street chapel in Lynn when I started going there. I left our Gaywood chapel because our Sunday school teacher, Mr Barrett, went as a missionary to the West Indies. We all cried when he left, he was such a good bloke. I picked on Tower Street because it had the best choir in the area, especially for young people. There were some smashing young girls in the choir and I was absolutely infatuated with one of them named Eileen Starr. She was like a Welsh beauty with masses of black hair and light eyes, but I didn't stand a cat in hell's chance with her because she was snooty and I'd never been out with anybody.

I was football mad. All my mates had girlfriends and I used to think to myself, I'll never get a girl. Then I did notice Gladys – she was Eileen's friend, and she was very pally with Eileen's brother Arthur. I was very pally with Arthur, too, so I asked Arthur if he would ask Gladys to come to the pictures with me. It was a terrible gloomy picture called *Somme*, about men dying by the million in the trenches, but we talked about it. Gladys's sister Flossie, who was fifteen years older than her, had been engaged to a man who died there. He'd been something in the Hatton Garden diamond market, then he'd gone to war and died. Later on Flossie had been engaged to another bloke, but he'd developed religious mania and gone to Manchester.

I knew Flossie through Sunday school. I took up teaching Sunday school when I moved to the Tower Street chapel, and Flossie was one of the superintendents. She was already into her thirties and a headmistress when I first knew her, and she was a soloist in the choir. Both she and Gladys belonged all their lives to the King's Lynn Musical Society, going all over the place to give recitals. One of the other superintendents at the Sunday school was a Mr Flowerday, whose son was another friend of Gladys's. Mr Flowerday had already lost two wives, poor man, and for years he wanted Flossie to marry him. They were always about together, at the chapel and outside it. He was the tailor who made all her clothes, for Flossie was such an awkward size she couldn't buy clothes in a shop. I don't think Flossie, being a headmistress, felt it was right to marry her tailor. He lived in her pocket, but she wouldn't consider him.

Because it had taken so long for me to notice Gladys, being so besotted with Eileen Starr, I didn't know I was putting someone else's nose out of joint by asking Gladys out. But there was a boy named Walter Frost in the choir who had noticed before I did just how smart and pretty Gladys was, like a bird with her head always held to one side or the other, her clothes always so neat and well-fitting. Walter Frost had seen what there was in Gladys long before I did and he didn't like it at all when I started going out with her. In fact he did everything in his power to try and part us. He knew everyone she knew, which I didn't – coming from Gaywood and, what's more, from a family of farmworkers and Primitive Methodists. Everyone Gladys knew, like Walter and the Starrs, were prosperous Lynn folk. All their parents knew each other, and their fathers were businessmen. They saw each other at the Lynn Theatre every week. Walter got Gladys's friend Ethel Harrod to try and part us, and Gladys would usually listen to Ethel because she was older and one of Flossie's friends even more than her own.

In the beginning I daresay Flossie didn't think it was right for Gladys to be courting an apprentice carpenter, but she was always straight and decent to me. I think Bertie, the brother, would have been the same, only I never had the chance of knowing him as a brother-in-law. He was smart and dapper like all the Towlers; the clothes they wore and the company they kept were a few of the ways I wasn't good enough for them. But poor Bertie died before I ever knew him. He married a girl named Nellie who worked at Donaldson's, the big fish and game shop in Lynn that took all the pheasants from Sandringham. Nellie had got Gladys a job there, about a year before I met her. Then she married Bertie, and not long after he was taken sick with a terrible nose bleed.

The doctors said it was some germ or other that Bertie had picked up while he was a prisoner of war in Germany that made his nose bleed and bleed. He'd been studying ladies' hairdressing in Rugby when the First World War broke out. Mr Towler had been intending to expand his business to include hairdressing for ladies (and today the shop where Gladys was born is a hairdresser's for men and women called Sizzers, without the old spiralling barber's sign outside), but the war put an end to Bertie's training. He'd been apprentice to a man with the unfortunate-sounding name of Meirholtz, and the very day war was declared someone from the town put a brick through the window. So Bertie came home and straightaway he enlisted in the Royal Warwickshires, and as soon as ever he joined the army he was captured by the Germans. He spent four years in a prison camp and he never went back to training as a ladies' hairdresser when he got home again. Then no sooner had he got married than he was taken to hospital – I went with Gladys to see him on the Saturday night and they had yards and yards of cotton wool up his nose, but it wouldn't stop bleeding. So he died.

Mr Towler made a tidy profit from his barbering business, and in his view an apprentice joiner wasn't good enough for Gladys. It used to break my mother's heart that Gladys would come regularly to our house for tea but I was never invited back to her home, for years. But just a few weeks after we started going out England were playing those Blue Devils at Wembley – Mr Towler might not have liked me but he liked football, and when Gladys asked his permission (as girls did, then) to go with me to the match, he couldn't say no.

Just a couple of weeks later we went to a fortune teller at the Mart, the big fair – one of the oldest in the country – that comes to the Market Place in Lynn every 14 February for ten days. Today there's no fortune teller, since the council banned them. Hunstanton is the nearest place to get your fortune told, when the fair goes there. Perhaps the people who live in Hunstanton have clearer heads on their shoulders because of the sea breezes blowing in. At any rate, their local council doesn't see any dangers in fortune telling.

The old gypsy woman who told fortunes when I was young was named Craig Watson and she was very well respected, more so than the wandering gypsies who would come around the lanes at odd times of the year. You could cross their palms with silver whenever you liked. Some of the men were tinkers and fortune telling was a sideline for the women. They would camp all over the place in those days – there weren't big gangs of them moving from place to place with the public objecting whenever a piece of land is found for them. The gypsies were poorer then, like most other people. You'd get a few camped here and there, ragged as can be, with none of those posh modern vans covered in chrome.

Gladys and I queued up outside Craig Watson's tent, and she went in first. I couldn't eavesdrop because of all the noise from the great steam engines and fairground organs. Then it was my turn. Inside the tent it was like another world, smelling of camphor and wet grass, and dark, with a crystal ball glowing on a table and Craig Watson's eyes above it. I was told to sit with my hands on the table in front of me. 'Your father rides a cycle on the roads, and he brings greens home from the allotment,' she said. My father had done that since before I was born, but what Craig Watson said next made the hair on the back of my neck stand up. 'You are going with a young lady whom you will one day marry. She's got golden streaks in her hair.' I thought to myself, I don't know whether she has or she hasn't. 'You will have an accident where there is machinery,' she finished.

Within six weeks I cut off the end of my thumb on a plane, but when I came out of the tent into the lights of the fairground I looked carefully at Gladys's hair to see if it had any golden streaks. It did.

When I cut the end of my thumb off the pain of it would bother me during the day when I was at work. Billy Hill, the builder I was doing my apprenticeship with, would tell me to hop it for half an hour to get some ice for it and I would go straight to Donaldson's. They had a terrific place at the back for making great blocks of ice. I would go to the chap on the machine and he would give me a bag of ice – then I would get word to Gladys in the office that I was there, and she would find some reason for coming out the back.

Soon it got so that we saw each other nearly every night. We would go to the pictures twice a week. We would walk for miles, talking. We would go on our bikes all around the villages that belonged to the royal estate. We would take picnics and watch the sun set – we saw some glorious sunsets. And that went on for nine years.

Her family's attitude to me changed completely when I became the man of the family – long before I married Gladys. Mrs Towler and Flossie had season tickets for the Walks ground, but the first time I ever went to a match with them was the day Mr Towler died. Poor Bertie had died just six weeks previously and the old man was in decline so I was invited to the house, which I never had been before, to stay there for a week over Christmas. We were coming away from a match on Boxing Day when old Mr Easter, who lived opposite the barber's shop, met us in the Walks to say that Mr Towler had just passed away. From then on there was nothing like me in the eyes of Mrs Towler and Flossie.

I don't think Gladys wanted to get married any more than I did, but after years of courting I was brought up with a shock one day. I thought, oh dear, I reckon I'll have to get married. It just came to me.

Yet even though Mrs Towler thought the world of me, and Flossie was always a good sort, when Gladys and I got engaged there was still the feeling that it was Gladys marrying me, not me marrying Gladys. It was not exactly as though her family and everyone she knew thought she was doing me a favour; I was never made to feel like some jumped-up parvenu – only like a Primitive Methodist or perhaps a poor relation. And it turned out so different from what might have been expected, because for all the years we were married Gladys took the best care of me that any man, any aristocrat, could ask for. I never lifted a finger in the house, never cleaned a grate, boiled an egg or washed a sock – Gladys did everything. Of course she wasn't happy at the prospect of living next door to my parents once we were married – she couldn't stand my father because he was so gloomy. Gladys was like Bertie, always so full of fun. She used to tell me, 'Len, I'll never look after your father, I couldn't stand to be moaned at all the time.' But when my mother died, Gladys cooked my father's meals and did his housework for years until the old man died too, and she did it without complaining once. But that was typical Gladys.

The night of my wedding, however, was the unhappiest night of my life. We went for our honeymoon to Eastbourne, and by the time we arrived it was dark and raining torrents. The window of our room looked out over the sea front and I remember looking out at the pier. It was all lit up, glittering in the rain, and I thought to myself, whatever have I done? It was a terrible night. Gladys was so ill that the whole side of her face swelled up like a hot potato. I was devastated. There was no sex that night, nor anything of the kind.

I'd been so worried about getting Highbury finished. My father wanted his house done first, so we did that, then I'd had just a few months to make mine ready for Gladys and me to move into after the wedding. I did every bit of the joinery and the fittings in both houses with my own hands, from the skirting boards to the ridge board at the top of the roof. I laid the floorboards and put in the rafters, every doorjamb, window frame and cupboard shelf, and the risers and the noses of every stair, the banisters and the picture rails – it went on and on, first the house for my parents, then Highbury. Gladys would come round in the evening to see what had been achieved during the day, but I worked on it round the clock. I would never do that again.

The morning of the day after our wedding the sun shone. Overnight there had been a great change. I woke next to Gladys and the thought was in my mind that there was no point in wishing it any other way, because I loved her. Her poor face stayed swollen up until we were on the train going home again, when something burst. She'd been so ill with it that we got off the train at King's Lynn still man and wife in name alone, but I knew we were going to be all right together. We never looked back.

8

My Two Great Loves: Part Two

G ladys left Donaldson's when we married but she went back there to work during the war. All the years between I was playing for Lynn Athletic and I reckon I was fitter at thirty-three than I had been at twenty – and I would make my head save my legs, I never chased a wasted ball. So I was picked at last to play for Lynn, and Flossie and Mrs Towler came to watch me play. But all the time I was playing for Lynn Gladys was working at Donaldson's again each Saturday because the war was on, so she couldn't come. She hardly ever saw me play for the town.

Playing for Lynn meant a lot to me, because I had had to fight hard for it. As soon as I had started work at fourteen, my father had moved heaven and earth to stop me playing football. I had got into the Gaywood team and my father would go around to see the secretary of the club to try and stop him picking me for a match. It upset me that my father did that, but I kept in the team and eventually I became captain.

It was the biggest disappointment of my life that I was never any good on the field. I was a better captain than I was a player. Later, when I became captain of Lynn Athletic, the best junior side in Lynn, it was the same – I had that ability of leadership, even imitating how the big club players took the field in those days, all running behind me as the captain with the ball. But I would much rather have been noted for my ability as a player.

When I finally got into the Lynn team, which I did by sheer perseverance and fitness, I never shone, and it was always the same thing that held me back – nerves. When we were practising in the evenings on the recreation ground I could beat them all; come the actual game, I was a load of rubbish.

It was the same with cricket. We would have cricket practice on the recreation ground and I was so promising that I was picked to play for Lynn first team. Matches were played on the Walks football ground at that time, and it's a beautiful ground, I'd say the most beautiful in the country, especially in summer with the trees that have grown to their prime all around it. I remember that day the sky was blue, it was hot but the trees were swaying in a breeze above the stands, and what my mother had done to my whites was a credit to her. Then I was put in to bowl – I was a fairly decent bowler – but that day I was no good at all. I was so bad I wasn't picked again. It was just nerves, but they stopped me giving my best. They closed me off from the rest of the world, isolated me like I was in a glass case – it was no way to play a team game. But no one was keener than me, my heart was in it, and even with my nerves in opposition to my legs I always got a game – outside the limelight I got a good game.

When I played football for Lynn they were in the Eastern Counties League, but being wartime we played the RAF teams as well, and the Observer Corps XI. It seemed like half the professional football players in England were in the Observer Corps and stationed in Norfolk. My lifelong friend Jack Savage, who had been best man at my wedding, was secretary of Lynn then. Every honour I've ever known in the football world I owe to him, but he was just like my father; he never gave me any credit – at least not to my face. The year I got into the team we reached the finals against Heacham – and he dropped me. He said, 'You ain't strong enough for them big buggers. They're too rough for you.' The bloke who took my place wasn't as good as me and I was back in the team the next week. But Savage was a tough man – he dropped his own son from the team on one occasion.

It was at the end of the second year I played for Lynn that I slipped on my ankle running after a ball and put my knee out of joint. For four months it was swollen up like nothing so much as a football. Then I was recommended to see a bone specialist in London who was familiar with sporting injuries. He was Denis Compton's bone doctor, amongst others. I can still hear the sound of it when the doctor got the joint to fit again – I heard it distinctly through the pain, like a cannon going off. 'That's what I wanted to hear,' said the doctor, smiling all over his face. But I never again walked without a limp, and I could never play football again.

I reckon that changed the course of my life – for a start it kept me out of the army. I was classified Grade 4 and kept on in my trade, and I think perhaps God meant me to have that injury because my nerves would have made me a terrible soldier, frightened to death. I was scared just going for the medical in Cambridge. I was so nervous that the doctor asked me, 'Are you like this on your own, Mr Rush? At home when you're reading a book?'

I said, 'No. And as soon as ever I leave here I'll be right as rain.'

I couldn't play football but the last thing I could do was give up the game: so straightaway I became an umpire and a referee. I had to pass the referees' test which was set by the bosses of the Lynn club – my mate Jack Savage, the chairman Mr Oliver Davidson and Mr Sid Collins. For plain devilment they turned my exam into an inquisition, firing every question under the sun at me – it went on for hours, and they laughed about it for years afterwards.

Some marvellous things happened to me after I took up refereeing. I didn't stop at being an ordinary referee – I became secretary of all the local referees and I brought their numbers up from fourteen to fifty-four. Then I was asked to represent

Norfolk referees on the Referees' Association of All England: six times a year I would go to London, to the Liberal Club behind Charing Cross Station, to spend the weekend. As if that wasn't enough, I was delighted to take on being secretary of the King's Lynn Football Club when my old friend Jack Savage gave it up. I went to Ipswich for meetings of all the League secretaries – Lynn was in the Eastern Counties League. All the London First Division teams like Tottenham, Arsenal and West Ham had very good A sides that competed in the Eastern Counties League, and I was very happy to get to know George Male through going to Ipswich. In his day, Male was a brilliant right fullback for Arsenal and England.

I would often go to Highbury Stadium to meet George when there was a match. On one particular occasion he wanted to show me round the stadium and the facilities. England was playing some foreign team down at Brighton, but for some reason George wasn't selected. The match wasn't played anyway, because the fog came rolling in from the sea and no one could see the ball or the goalposts. Instead, all the England team came up to the Arsenal to do some training there, and they arrived whilst I was with George in the changing rooms. We said hello to everyone, and I was wondering where Stanley Matthews was. More than anyone I wanted to meet Matthews, having watched every single game he'd played for England. But he wasn't there. I wanted to wait around, but George said, 'Come on, Len, let's go and have a look around the ground.'

There was a lone figure on the pitch, one man doing some training by himself. It was Stan Matthews.

'There's old Stan,' said George. 'Let's go and have a word with him.'

We walked over and I was introduced. Matthews must have realised how pleased I was to meet him because a couple of days later I got through the post the marvellous big photograph that hangs on my breakfast room wall, signed right across. I told the Queen the story of how I met Matthews, and she said she'd always admired him, but of course she's shaken hands with him more than once.

When I was secretary of the Norfolk referees and the Lynn club everyone said I was the best secretary they had ever had. Without boasting at all, I was really heart and soul in it then, and I knew a lot because I was so interested. Gladys helped tremendously, typing out all the minutes. One time we had a player named Norman Rowle who was very good and some of the bigger clubs were after him. Derby asked me to take him there for a trial, so I took him with another lad, and they said they wanted to sign Norman on. But they wanted to sign him on and leave it at that. I wanted some money – not much, a couple of hundred quid – and I wanted Derby to send a team down to Lynn for a friendly game. I was persistent, and in the end they gave us some money and they sent a team to play Lynn. Norman played for the Derby A team for some years, and then he came back and played for Lynn. He carries the coffins now, for the undertaker.

Shortly after that trip to Derby the call came: would I be a scout for Derby in East Anglia? Gladys didn't stand in my way. What I liked best was being sent to see a game, to watch a particular player, and spotting another one while I was there. Sometimes I would have to go right out into the wilds to little villages in the middle of nowhere.

When I was appointed a life member of the Norfolk County Football Association I couldn't believe it. I would attend the annual meeting of the FA and mix with all the big names of football. At matches I would sit next to celebrities like Jimmy Essen, Charles Buchan and Clem Stevenson. I was invited to be a steward at the Cassius Clay fight against Henry Cooper at Wembley. I was put on the main gate where all the famous people came through, and then for the fight itself I was given a seat just three yards from the ring. And I was a steward at the World Cup in the year when England won.

I ask myself why I didn't get my living by football when I had the chance. I ought to have become secretary to one of the bigger League clubs that had professional secretaries. You never hear of a League secretary being given the boot – it's always the manager that carries the can – yet it's the secretary who has as much to do as anyone with signing on new players and building the team. But my trouble was that I was enjoying what I was doing, and not thinking of it as work.

And of course I had the pigeons to care for, too. I'd always spent a lot of time with them, and now, despite all my activity behind the scenes in the world of football, because I'd stopped being a player it was the birds that moved to the centre of my life. And where Gladys and I had previously shared a passion for football – and indeed were still to do so, to a certain extent – now all our lives together were to be shared with the birds.

9

The Queen's New Flight

The first young birds I bred from the handful I'd brought from Sandringham to start the new Royal Lofts at Highbury were the beauties I'd hoped for. I'd mated their parents later than usual because the weather stayed Siberian right into February that year. But then out came the nest boxes – little dowelling-fronted cupboards big enough for two pigeons and two nest bowls, should you want the second batch of eggs to be hatched by the same birds – and the day was set aside for overseeing the pairing of the birds and settling them into a new domestic routine as wedded couples.

The nest boxes had been brought from Sandringham with the birds since pigeons are possessive of them – or rather, the cocks are. Using their old nest boxes gave me a better chance of a happy loft with my new birds. Having been separated and celibate since the start of winter, pigeons should always be very amenable to the whole operation, but to be sure there are no squabbles my habit is to take only one pair at a time and see to their comfort. First I put the cock into the nest box, *his* nest box, then I bring the hen I've chosen to him and introduce her to her mate.

In my mind's eye I can see the squabs they will produce, and so can the birds: straightaway the cock struts around showing off the shine on his feathers by blowing out his crop and cooing in a deep and fruity voice while the hen leads him on. The cock goes round and round in circles and the hen seems to walk away from him – but even outside the confines of the nest box she wouldn't go very far. Soon she's following *him*, and when the cock stands still she'll gently stroke the back of his head with her beak. Everything is going swimmingly. She offers herself to him, turning round, and he hops up and treads her.

So much for gentleness. What follows is the driving of the hen to the nest by the cock. Whenever they are out of the nest box the cock charges after his bride, buffeting her with his wings, pecking at her head, forcing her back to the nest box and refusing to take no for an answer right until the first egg is laid. In the nest box itself there are intervals of billing and cooing and more treading during this period, which ensures that the second egg is fertile – there are nearly always two glossy white eggs to a brood, each about an inch and a half long. The first one appears in the nest bowl about eight days after the first treading. Pigeons don't make much of a fuss about their nests. In the wild they will throw together odds and ends of straw, feathers, bits of string – anything that comes to beak. I supply them with clean sawdust in a pottery nest bowl, which I put in the nest box when the hen is eggy.

She lays the first egg between five and six in the afternoon and the second should arrive on schedule around two in the afternoon of the next day but one – always blunt end first. Egg sitting doesn't start until the second egg is laid, because the eggs want to hatch at almost the same time. If they didn't, the second, smaller, chick might well be bullied to death by its big brother or sister. The birds have a schedule for sitting, too. They have an agreement built into their genes whereby the cock has a turn of duty by day, almost office hours, and the hen sits the evening and the night through to the cock's clocking-on time the next morning. For eighteen days this routine is followed; then the ugly little squabs start pecking through their shells, usually the second-laid first. A tapping sound can be heard in the egg a good seven hours before the first chip is made in the shell – the little creature inside has become cramped for space and its larder is empty, so it uses the sharp little horn growing on its upper beak, its egg tooth, to make perforations all around the blunt end of its shell and push it off. The egg tooth quickly disappears, absorbed into its beak, as the chick finds its parents' open beaks and feasts on the pigeon milk waiting there to nourish it.

Before they are nine days old the birds have to be ringed, otherwise their feet will have grown too large to pass through the ring. You might as well toss an unringed bird out into the wild to fend for itself, because in order to race a bird has to be ringed, like a baby has to be registered. The rings are issued and recorded by the Royal Pigeon Racing Association in Cheltenham in January – nearly two million every year.

Once the pigeon milk is used up, the parent birds will soften grain in their crops for the young birds to feed on until they're ten days old. Then regular hard grain is pumped into the ever-open beaks of the nestlings for another couple of weeks, by which time the youngsters are covered in feathers and nosing about the loft ready to peck at turkey pellets and little grains of wheat. Sometimes they're reluctant to feed themselves, having had it so easy, and you have to step in and feed them by hand, because if a young bird goes without food for a day the development of the feathers is disrupted. A fret mark will crease one of the flight feathers, or a sort of tide mark will appear across the plumage. You might have to dunk a young bird's beak into water to get it to drink for itself, which it soon will, like a horse, sucking the water down. As soon as the young are weaned they're put into a compartment of their own to learn to live together – and fly together.

By the time a bird is six weeks old it will have all its feathers and it will be ready to learn to fly. If you open the sliding doors of the loft the birds will hop out on to the grass and wander around in the open, tasting it. One day they'll have sufficient strength to fly on to the traps, and they'll sit there a bit. After about a week, up they go – and you're wondering and wondering where they're going to land, because you want them to land in your loft. You're rattling the corn in the tin can and sending telepathic messages to them: 'Land in the loft! Land in the loft!' Usually all goes well – you see the youngsters circling in the sky above the loft and then coming down when they're told to, into the loft.

Then comes the day, a couple of weeks after they were first let out, that they fly off. Instead of circling over the loft as if they were scared to let it out of sight, they'll all keep flying in one direction until you can't see them any more, and you don't see them for maybe a couple of hours, no matter how hard you stare at the sky. Then suddenly they'll zoom down from another direction. They've been ranging the countryside, and they've found their way back to the one little rectangle of roof that is the loft – just one little rectangle amongst the patchwork of roofs and gardens that fills the spaces between the roads, and it doesn't matter if the roof of the loft is painted stripes of bright orange and purple or left a dull-brown felt colour. In that small feathered head there's obviously brain enough to recognise the landmarks for miles around the loft. I imagine what they can see as they take to their wings around mine: the Gayton Road just a hundred yards from the loft streaking out over the hill to the countryside in one direction, cutting into the town in the other to become part of a maze that's full of moving cars and buses and lorries grinding along at a pathetic pace. Then, straight and clear as steel, the railway cuts through, and where it stops now it used to go on, as the bird must be able to tell from the leftover traces, straight and green, to the royal station at Wolferton and on to Heacham and Hunstanton.

A pigeon can see the whole of the Sandringham estate at a glance, and by turning its head it can see the Wash, whether the tide is in or the sandbanks are bare to the sky and speckled with seals. The saltmarshes must be full of interest, full of life, a knobbly craze of green hugging the coast from Hunstanton down to Lynn from the east, and all the way from Boston in the west. And there at Lynn is the Cut. It was hand-made over two miles by men with spades, their horses and carts toiling in the mud to open up the Wash to the merchants of the town. A straight waterway glinting in the sun is nothing unusual to my birds. Inland there's the Great Ouse wiggling south, but it's joined by other so-called rivers that are drawn with a ruler over miles and miles, all the way from Cambridgeshire and what used to be called Huntingdonshire. And what will be of special interest to my birds, since they'll fly the North Road when they're old enough, is the great fan of small, straight roads that radiate out from the elbow of the Wash, from Boston all the way round to Wisbech, as striking a feature as any to be found on a map of the English countryside and as distinct as a map to a bird's eye.

The Queen never came to the lofts when the birds were busy rearing their young. By the time she came to see the pigeons in the winter the characters of all the young ones from the year before would be clear – which ones were bossy, and which were going to be content with a lower perch. In each batch of young there would be a leader, the first one to hop out on to the grass in the spring, the first to spread its wings – most likely a winner in young bird races. By the time the Queen paid her second visit to Highbury the young ones had raced for a season.

Young birds, however, aren't completely reliable until they're past yearlings. You race them in special young bird races and you're pleased when they win, as several of the Queen's did that first year, but the races are only up to a couple of hundred miles. You can't trust a young bird to fly the long distances. Some will manage it, like the hen bred by the Middle East Pigeon Service in the last war that flew five hundred miles back to its loft in Cairo, two hundred and eighty of them over water, at six and a half months old. But you expect a fair number of young birds to fall by the wayside on short races, even on training tosses. The stamina and courage needed for long-distance flying are qualities the flyer develops in his birds through training, and it's not until a bird is a year old that you can tell how much potential it's got.

The bird progresses thereafter, up to four or five years old, and then it declines – most of a loft's long-distance winners are between two and five years old. For a long time, though, the holder of the British thousand-mile record was a small yearling red chequered hen that escaped from its RAF loft in Gibraltar to get home to Gillingham in Kent where it was hatched, 1,090 miles away, in fourteen days. And on the other hand there was a six-year-old cock named Alfonso that won the Manchester Flying Club's first San Sebastian race, a distance of over seven hundred miles. There will always be exceptional birds to make nonsense of broad statements of fact.

The average lifespan of a bird, for instance, is ten to twelve years – yet there was one old blue bar hen I brought from West Newton that was twenty-four years old, and she was a wonderful old matron. She couldn't be sold at that age and I couldn't bear the idea that her neck might be wrung, so she moved to the lofts at Highbury where she settled down as a foster mother with all the ease of a young bird. She was the *grande dame* of the lofts, and lucky enough to be free of the rheumatics that so many of the Delmotte-Jurions suffer from. She had war memories of flying in RAF bombers over Europe. She'd bred a winner of the North Road Championship from Lerwick for Steele. She was the only bird at Highbury still to have the cipher GVI on her ring from having been hatched during King George VI's reign, and the Queen would have been introduced to her first when she visited the lofts with her father as a child.

She was still alive the second year the Queen came to visit her pigeons, though that day ended in tragedy. There were nearly a hundred birds in the lofts by then and the young birds were back in the same compartments with their parents, although since it was winter the fathers were in one compartment with their sons and the mothers in another with their daughters.

The Queen came alone with Lady Mary Morison in the car, and she and I went almost straightaway down the garden to see the birds. I was amazed at the Queen's memory, how she recognised the old birds from the year before – and apart from being a little gawky, like adolescents will be, there was little to tell the young birds from their parents. I told her about a hen that was missing because she insisted on spending the winter back at the old lofts in West Newton.

The Queen enquired if she would come back in the spring to start another brood.

'Nothing would stop her,' I said. 'She'll want her mate then. Sometimes I think I see her in the sky even now, checking out the lofts to see if her mate is ready. She's a good bird and one of her young was a winner this last summer from Berwick-on-Tweed. A young cock,' and I picked up the bird because we were in with the cocks, 'this one.'

He was a fine blue chequered cock, and from the start he'd been very strong and healthy and beautiful. I had another reason for showing him to the Queen – one of the special things about him was his eye.

'Look at his eyes, Your Majesty,' I said, holding the young cock up so that she could see. The cock had orange-coloured eyes, which is the most common colour, although the orange can verge on red or brown, or it might be so dark as to seem black, or so pale that it's yellowy white. But this was a good bright orange eye. 'You can see a line around the pupil there, within the iris. You see it's a violet colour, just outside the pupil itself – that's the eye sign. Some people call it the circle of correlation because they say you can tell from it how good a racer the bird is.'

The Queen noticed that I didn't sound as though I really

believed this, and said so. I told her I wasn't sure that I did, but that I wouldn't deny a chap his hobby horse. 'There's one man I know from Leeds,' I went on, 'who makes a living going around to different lofts and looking a flyer's birds in the eye. For a few quid he'll sort out the racers and the breeders and say which of both will be successful, all by looking at the eye sign. It might be a violet line like this, or it might be black, white, blue, green or yellow. It might be thick or thin, or it might be serrated. As a rule you need a hefty magnifying lens to tell, but this young cock has such a strong eye sign you can see it just by looking. According to the theory, anyway, he's a champion in the making. The basket will tell. I'll send him to the far north of Scotland later this year and then we'll know.'

The Queen wished him luck and wanted to be introduced to the other hopefuls for the coming old bird racing season. The royal birds would be undertaking a full racing calendar for the first time from their new lofts. The young cocks were especially promising, I told her. There was one, No. 77, that had the blood of a North Road Champion from Banff in him by his dam and that of a three-time winner from Perth by his sire, and I believed he was set to be a credit to them. He was a mealy, and when you held him he felt so corky you'd think he had the strength to fly home from Timbuktu. Berwick is the longest race for the young birds from Lynn and No. 77 hadn't performed marvellously in that, but he'd won from Hull and that was enough to give me hopes for him.

We went through into the hens' compartment so that the Queen could see the mate I had chosen for this particular mealy – one of the old birds. The mate she'd had the year before was the grandfather of one of the young hens and I wanted to breed them together – grandfather/granddaughter is a good mating for in-breeding (which in pigeons is a good thing rather than a bad one). It gave me the chance of putting the old hen which had proved herself a marvellous breeder with the fresh young cock.

The Queen and I talked at length about the finer points and advantages of in-breeding and cross-breeding, and I explained why I wanted the blood of the grandfather and his grand-daughter to mix. Since I already had in the lofts a distinct family of birds I didn't need to practise a great deal of in-breeding to establish my own family, either of a young bird with its ancestor, be it parent or grandparent, or through a sideways relationship, such as brother, sister, niece, nephew, cousin, between mates. But sometimes there are points in a pigeon that a flyer will want to magnify through in-breeding, and the granddaughter in this case deserved to be magnified because she was so promising.

Looking at all the birds was a more complicated job than it had been the year before, but more exciting, too, since the young ones were set to breed the third generation in the lofts. The Queen had a last word with the *grande dame* of the lofts, the twenty-four-year-old, and we went back into the cocks' loft. Just as we were about to leave that and go back to the house, the Queen said, '*She* shouldn't be in here.' It was the old hen, in the cocks' loft. I don't know how she had managed to follow us through to it. 'You're right, Your Majesty,' I said. I needed both hands to open the door because it was a new one I had just built and it wasn't fixed in its runners yet. 'Come along, my beauty,' I said to the hen, to keep her close to the door while I opened it to let her through to the hens' compartment. It was a good solid door, about six feet tall and very heavy. As I was trying to open it, it fell inward right across the loft.

I thank God it missed the Queen – though only by inches. It missed me as I tried to catch it. But it fell on ten or more cocks that were strutting around on the floor showing off to the Queen, and it fell on the old hen. The cocks made such haste to avoid it hitting them they squawked out in all direc-tions before the door crashed down its full length across the floor. The air was thick with sawdust and feathers flying all over the place and there was a terrible commotion from the startled birds, but under the door was the old hen.

We carried her back to the house, still alive but barely conscious – that she should have lived so long to die like this. Blood dripped slowly from her beak and there was blood on my hands from where she was cut on her body – blood on my hands, I thought. Gladys found a shoebox and some fresh muslin to make a hospital nest for her but there was nothing we could do, only wait for her to die. The Queen was so dismayed. She tried to sound encouraging and she stroked the old bird's head. I was expecting the hen to give up the ghost as we looked at her, but she lived for two whole days before she finally died.

Gladys made some fresh coffee and we sat by the fire in the parlour with the hen quiet in her nest on the table. To take our minds off her the Queen asked about a painting on the wall beside the fireplace: it showed a man with strong arms tying a sheaf of corn at harvest time. It pleased me that she asked about it because it had belonged to my mother – it was by a local artist and the man in the picture was my mother's brother, my Uncle Jim, who in his day was a horseman and a champion ploughman. I was glad the Queen had changed the subject like that, but that was typical of her. It was so easy to be with her, and there was never any awkwardness. She always knew the right thing to say.

I spared the Queen the details of other tragedies, such as smashes – the term we flyers give to races when unexpected bad weather means that many fine birds never get home. But when she came to the lofts I would tell her which birds were missing and how many youngsters had gone off. Despite the losses, however, the lofts were soon fully stocked with birds I'd bred from the West Newton Delmotte-Jurions, and the time came when I wanted new stock to cross with them. I had my eye on some C. J. Williams birds, which are like the Belgian birds – in fact a long-cast pigeon, with a very dark blue in their plumage. They don't have a deep keel like a boat, but are firm in front and straight-backed, with the tail held down like it should be.

I told the Queen what I had in mind. The next thing I knew the Queen had told the Queen Mother, who for years has been a friend of the great racehorse breeder and pigeon fancier C.J. Williams. Mr Williams insisted on giving the Queen a dozen of his best birds for the Highbury lofts. He sent them in a horse box to the Jockey Club at Newmarket, from where I picked them up.

The majority of winners of classic races over the last hundred years have been the product of the first cross on a good line-bred family – the Sandringham birds were my line-bred family, and now I had a cross in time to breed with my birds that very year. The next year the Queen would be able to see the young birds that were the result.

After I became Royal Lofts manager we could never tell anyone when the Queen was due to come to Highbury, so Gladys and I just had to hope we would have no unexpected callers at the same time. The year after the Queen had seen the young birds resulting from the cross of the C.J. Williams birds I was looking forward to showing her one of them again, an old bird now, that had won the Thurso race from the very far north of Scotland. Half an hour before the appointed time, though, there was a knock on the front door.

'Who can that be?' I said to Gladys, feeling a bit put out.

I opened the front door, to find the Queen standing on the doorstep.

'Don't worry, Mr Rush,' she said, 'we're early.'

We left Gladys and the lady-in-waiting in the parlour because I was keen to get to the lofts and so was the Queen – she always was. I straightaway showed her No. 87, the C.J. Williams cross that had won the Federation cup from Thurso. It was a beautiful sleek red chequered cockbird and the Queen took it from my hands and held it for herself.

'I thanked the Queen Mother for arranging for the birds to be sent by Mr Williams when I saw her in the summer, Your Majesty,' I said, 'but I hope you will tell her what a fine bird this is and that it's won for you.'

As she stroked the bird's head the Queen said of course she would. Thurso is as far north in Scotland as you can go on the mainland, as far north as John O'Groats to the east of it and Cape Wrath to the west. It was a good result for a yearling, and I now had the problem of deciding whether to send him on another long race or to keep him safe over shorter distances to be sure of retaining him in the loft for breeding. We discussed the matter at length. There were four youngsters in the loft which I'd already bred from him; their dam was one of the younger pure Delmotte-Jurions. I was thinking of mating him this coming year with his grandmother, so we looked at the youngsters and the grandmother, and we talked and talked.

The Queen asked me if No. 87 was likely to perform even better as a two-year-old.

'You can feel how fit he is, Your Majesty. And he's got the mentality – you get the feel of that through holding him, too – that he won't be diverted by anything short of an electrical storm.' In reply to her enquiry I assured her that he had been trained over water. 'I take all the birds down below myself whenever I can, Your Majesty, on my mate's fishing smack. Then I send them round to Skegness on the other side of the Wash – I send them there twice, to be sure they'll take the Wash for granted when they reach it after a long flight – that they won't hesitate to cross it.'

'Well, I leave the decision to you, Mr Rush, whether to send him to Thurso again or not – he's a marvellous creature.'

I agreed. 'We couldn't do it,' I said. 'Just recently I was down below, and there was only one man on deck, steering the boat – old Sammy, a brother of one of the Boneses, the big fishing people of North End. That was a journey right out into the Wash, and there's nothing to do until you get to the prawning grounds – we were all sitting down below, laughing and talking, when Sammy called, "Up here! Up here!" We rushed up, and in the distance there was something bobbing up and down. We heaved to and went right up to it – and there was a young boy and a young girl, two students in a canoe. They'd come all the way down from Scotland on the rivers and they were crossing the Wash to Lynn. But the Wash is deadly. They would never have made it to Lynn in that little canoe – they had all the charts for the journey, but they would still have been drowned. We heaved them on board, boat as well, and they had to stay with us all day. We brought them up at night to the quayside in Lynn, then they took their canoe on a train the next morning to get to Lincolnshire. They were lucky old Sammy saw them. A fit pigeon stands a lot more chance of getting across the Wash than they ever did.'

I told Her Majesty that a lot of flyers were now winning races on what was called the widowhood system. It made it hard for people like me who believed in racing the natural way, because we needed better and better birds in order to compete with them.

The Queen hadn't heard of the widowhood system, so I explained it to her. 'The Continentals did it first, Your Majesty,' I said, 'like everything else. Only the cocks race. The hens stay home, and you don't even train them. You pair your cocks up and let them breed one round of youngsters, then the hens lay the second round of eggs and after that you take the hens far enough away so the cocks can't even hear them. The cock birds will be on the eggs all week, then say you're sending your pigeons away on the Friday, you go down to the cocks' loft and take the hen birds with you, one by one, and you put the hen in with her mate. The hen is fed first, so she's only got her mate on her mind when she sees him. Well, of course, they go mad – but you don't let them tread at all. As soon as they attempt that, you whip the cock away.' I remembered I was talking to the Queen. 'It takes their strength away, don't it?' I said in a hurry. 'You grab that cock bird and put it in the basket. In the marking place you can tell which ones are widowed because there's fights galore with the cocks. But when they go home they go like bullets.

'Everyone's winning on the widowhood, I'm sorry to say. Some of the widowed cocks are kept in darkness once the race season starts, with music piped in to keep them calm and rested – then thirty seconds with the hen and into the basket. When the cocks get back some flyers *still* don't allow the hens to be shown to them for more than thirty seconds, poor things. Some are allowed half an hour or an hour together before the hens are taken up the garden to another loft, out of sight, out of earshot.

'It's a completely different way of managing a loft, Your Majesty. It has a whole lot of special requirements – special nest boxes you can get the hens into and the cocks out from so fast the birds must be dizzy from it. You need a special loft, come to that. Then there are special baskets for carrying them because they fight so, special feed mixes, tonics. But what you *don't* need with widowhood so much is the training, which I suppose makes it attractive to a lot of flyers. It's enough that the cocks are mad to see their hens again.'

The Queen rightly assumed that her birds would not be raced on the widowhood system. She asked what the birds were fed that was so different from the food a normal racing pigeon was given, and if it really worked.

'Your Majesty,' I told her, 'a pigeon corn merchant will try and sell you a Widowhood Mix, a Moulting Mix, a Squeaker Mix, a Winter Mix, a Miracle-Super-Plus Mix. Everyone agrees you can't race pigeons on anything but the best – you couldn't just go down the farm and get some corn to feed them, then expect them to win. But no one agrees on what the best might be. People feed their birds on all manner of things: tic beans and maple peas, acorns and sunflower seeds, dun beans and maize, wheat, barley, oats, polished rice, dari and hemp seeds. You might throw in blood, fish and meat meal, milk, buttermilk and whey. Some people swear by kaffir corn and buckwheat with cabbage and dried yeast, vetches and tares, wheat pollards and beech mast. And different times of year you feed them different mixes — different times of the week you feed them differently, too, depending on the races. People spend hours deciding which grains to give and how much of each, weighing them out, mixing them. I never feed the birds a patent mix — I give them barley and maize and maple peas, with sunflower seeds for titbits, when they come in from a race. Then I give them vitamins, but none of these drugs you can buy that are supposed to be remedies for everything under the sun, nor the potions that are supposed to put a shine on the bird's feathers. Grit and salt and minerals are what they need.'

The Queen pleased me by saying how very fit the birds all looked. 'I daresay most of the mixtures are superfluous if only some common sense is used in caring for the birds,' she added.

Then I told her how I wished I'd opened a shop that sold everything racing pigeons need. 'If I had my time over again,' I told her, 'I wouldn't go into the building trade, I'd be a shopkeeper.' With Gladys's business abilities, I assured her, I'd probably have gone on to open a second shop, selling footballs and cricket bats. But it was Gladys, really, who stopped me from opening even one shop, because she didn't want to know anything that was tied. She remembered her father always at his barber's shop fifty-two weeks of the year. 'But Gladys helps me run my carpentry business instead so I shan't complain. In all my married life I've never signed a cheque.'

The Queen laughed. She got on well with Gladys — they would chat together like old friends, like only two women can.

When we went back into the house Gladys was still talking to Lady Susan Hussey, the Queen's lady-in-waiting, in the parlour, so we joined them there. The Queen sat down on the sofa by the window and Lady Susan was on the armchair beside the fire. We had coffee. We were talking all together and none of us heard anyone knocking on the front door. There came a tapping on the window behind the Queen's head. She turned around and came face to face with one of the Miss Gotobeds, two unmarried sisters who lived in a bungalow opposite – they were very alike to look at, and they would dress alike, right down to a green umbrella for the rain, and I can't remember which Miss Gotobed had come calling.

Both the Miss Gotobeds had a way with them that made you feel impatient, even before they'd said anything. 'Fusspots,' Gladys would say. They were members of our Gaywood chapel. It amazed me they could remember the day for services was Sunday, the way they would forget everything else – the number of times they would ask Gladys about the arrangements for the Missionary Circle, the Women's Fellowship and the Guild, when they were just as regular as Sunday services. If there was just one neighbour that didn't know the Queen had come to our house, it was one or the other Miss Gotobed.

'I think one of your neighbours wants you, Mrs Rush,' said the Queen.

I got up from where I sat by the dining table and I could see Miss Gotobed. She was holding on to the windowsill with her head just above it – the house stands higher at the back – and she was staring at the Queen like a rabbit frozen by a light. To come across the Queen at such close quarters when she was expecting to see only Gladys and me must have given her a bad shock!

10

Theory and Practice of Racing Pigeons

Once I asked the Queen, when she arrived at our house, 'Your Majesty, what about your chauffeur?' I thought perhaps he ought to come inside, in the warm.

The Queen smiled and told me he was perfectly all right and had gone for a little walk. He must have come to know Gaywood well over the years, and the neighbours must have come to know him. It was marvellous how they all knew the Queen had arrived even though I had never told them she was coming. There were always people waiting at their garden gates to see her come out of the house again, to say goodbye to Gladys and me and get into her car.

Remembering the unfortunate episode of the planned first visit, when half Gaywood turned out because of my indiscretion, I lived in dread of someone getting to know beforehand that she was coming. Once when I went out to meet the Queen's car I noticed out of the corner of my eye a photographer crouched down low on the pavement by next door's privet hedge, camera to his eye, clicking away. I was never aware of the police stationed nearby whenever the Queen came, although of course they had to be there, but that photographer was soon sent packing.

'Don't worry, Mr Rush,' said the Queen, seeing the dismay on my face because of the photographer. She was more concerned about me being upset than about the man himself.

When he could have been holding a gun instead of a camera, I was saying to myself, but God preserve us from such a thing ever happening.

Being Royal Lofts manager I was all of a sudden a celebrity, and I was invited to no end of dos. I was asked to judge pigeon shows and speak at Rotary Clubs and Federation dinners all over the country. Every month Gladys would type out an account of my expenses for me to send to Sandringham, and a cheque would arrive from Mr Pillar the next day. He and Major Fellowes were going to come and look at my books from when I first started, but they never came – they trusted me. At Christmas a man would arrive on the doorstep with a plum pudding from Sandringham, and there would be a brace of pheasants every year.

Gladys saw me on television once when I was judging show birds in a competition organised by the *People* newspaper. She'd just finished some ironing and turned on the television and there I was, at home in our parlour but inside the television. Gladys thought it was very funny. Show birds have been bred far longer than racing birds. Pigeons shows were held two hundred years ago, even before there were dog shows or cattle and livestock shows, because in the days before railways the birds were so much easier to move about. Much later they stopped showing in taverns and held big shows in the Crystal Palace in south London. So the standards for show birds are well established and a judge has to go very strictly by a detailed description of the head, beak, wattle, eye, cere, neck, legs, feet, body, shape, carriage, size, feathering, colour, flights, tail and any special features such as crests, frills, muffs, beards, helmets, masks, hoods, slippers or grizzlings. So many points are awarded for each.

I was glad I was a racing pigeon man, because there is no standard as such for show homers – they just have to look good and feel good to the eye and the hand. Show birds have to conform. Pouters, for instance, have to be able to blow out

1 *The man with the tin can when young. The blue bar hen eating from the tin can is one of the birds I bred from Baldwin and Bad Luck in my first lofts, a lean-to behind our house in Gaywood.*

2 *Cutting flowers for my mother in front of our house*

3 *A courting couple; Gladys in her flapper's dress*

4 *Sunday suits for Sunday schools. I'm the teacher.*

5 *Wedding day. Flossie is maid of honour; my cousin, Ted Neal, is best man;
Gladys's bridesmaid is Miss Clarke.*

6 *My birds being trained to cross water. They don't like water but being tossed
from a boat in the middle of the Wash gives them no choice but to cross it.*

7 *Mr Walter Jones, the first Royal Lofts manager, outside the lofts at West Newton with King George VI and family*

8 *The new Royal Lofts at the end of my garden, a change of lifestyle for the Queen's birds*

9 *The birds go happily into the basket for their first training toss*

10 *A mystery ride along the Norfolk roads on the front of my butcher's boy bike*

11 *We reach Castle Rising and the birds bolt homewards without anyone telling them the way*

12 *Cash prizes were sent to Sandringham but I kept the cups*

13 The Fur and Feathers Show at Sandringham, always an opportunity for a chat with the Queen Mother

14 *Captain of the Gaywood team –
before the football pitch was sold off in
building lots. I bought one of the lots
and built my house there.*

15 *The FA Cup at the Royal Garden
Hotel in Kensington to celebrate its
100th anniversary. A wonderful day in
my life.*

16 *Her Majesty arriving at our house in Gaywood. I am waiting by the gate,
but a neighbour is caught by surprise.*

17 *An hour later, the Queen leaves*

18–19 Pigeons at home and abroad (in Trafalgar Square). Wherever I go, I look for strays amongst the street pigeons, but there's never a ringed leg to be seen.

20 *The old birds gossiping together on the perches above their nest boxes*

21 *Two lovely, comfortable squabs in their nest boxes*

*22 A bird leaves my hands outside the Norfolk Gates of Sandringham. It will
reach home in Gaywood before me.*

their crop to twice the diameter of their body, as though they're trying to blow their own head off. The show carrier is supposed to have a walnut-shaped wattle at the base of its beak which is too large for it to see to fly, added to which it's supposed to have eye ceres over an inch across, which on the correct (for carriers) long, narrow skull stand out like carnations on either side of its head – with the walnut wattle between. Not many show birds are grotesque, though. Mainly they're very beautiful, such as the Satinette and the Turbiteen with their frills, the Jacobin with its hood and the Fantail with its forty tail feathers. But it was the racing world I became more involved in than ever one I was pitchforked into stardom as Royal Lofts manager.

The very first time I spoke in public was when I'd just been appointed. I was invited to a dinner in London organised by Colin Osman of the weekly paper the *Racing Pigeon*, and when I got there Colin said, 'I want you to speak.' There were five hundred people there, half in one room and half in another, with a microphone for me so that all of them could hear. It was like when I played football in a big match – I was all of a sudden oblivious to anyone being there at all. I didn't see anybody or hear anybody, but instead of being betrayed by my nerves as I always was on the football field I found I could speak like my natural self to all those people listening. I got a tremendous write-up in the paper. I think all those years of teaching Sunday school had stood me in good stead, and I must have got over my nerves about speaking in public years before in the chapel.

Back home in Lynn I had also become famous. The neighbours talked about me. People greeted me in the street when I didn't know them – but they knew me. The birds I carried on the front of my bike down to the Flying Club for marking-up night weren't ordinary birds, and I would have to discuss what their chances of winning might be with complete strangers who had probably never so much as looked at a racing pigeon before, let alone fancied one. They would peer at the birds through the feeding holes in their basket as though they were looking for gold. I could see lots of questions forming on the tips of peoples' tongues that they couldn't bring themselves to ask: What's she *really* like, the Queen? Does she feel at home in your front room? Does she have a cup of tea?

Fanciers, I'm glad to say, are a more straightforward bunch of people. Anyway, I knew everyone in the Flying Club like they knew me, and the royal birds had been flying with the club since it started, even before there were racing clocks or rubber race rings. Then a number would be stamped in coloured marking ink on the bird's wing on marking-up night, and only the secretary would know what it was. When the bird got home telegrams were sent to the club secretary giving the time of a bird's arrival at its loft and its race number, or the flyer would rush as fast as his feet would carry him to the yard at the Swan where the secretary would be waiting for news, to take down the times of the members' birds and check the numbers given against his records from marking-up night. It wasn't easy to cheat. With the sponsorship of national races that's come with recent times there's more incentive to cheat, but since the introduction of the clock it's even harder.

Clocks were an expensive piece of equipment when they were first introduced from Belgium at the turn of the century, costing the then high price of £5–7 each – a price that stayed the same until around 1950, and perhaps later. Nowadays, with inflation, the manufacturer doesn't even give the price in his advertisements because it might have gone up by the time the advertisement reaches the fancier in the pigeon press. But the cheapest is nearly £250, and a good one is nearer £400. You can buy computerised clocks now that flash numbers at you in lights as though the art of reading a dial was lost, along with the art of calculating velocities with pencil and paper. The computerised clock you can only read with the aid of another computer – on its own it's as much use as an electric toaster for timing in your birds.

There were all manner of ready reckoners available for club secretaries in the days when each bird's velocity was worked out by hand on a huge pad of paper. It shouldn't be difficult to work out, you'd think, being no more than very long division: the distance flown divided by the time taken to fly it. But the time taken is known to the second, so the distance flown is converted to sixtieths of a yard to make sense of the sum, and on race night the secretary would sit there dividing tens of millions of sixtieth parts of yards by tens of thousands of seconds. He or his wife got extremely good at it, but the business of calculating racing velocities had only begun – on checking with the master timer it might emerge that the racer's clock was set slow and opened fast, or it might have been set fast and opened slow, or it might have been set slow and opened still slower, or vice versa. All sorts of little problems of this kind had to be taken into account.

The secretary would reach for his Lightning Calculator (price one shilling post free) that gave clock variations at a glance, but even so it would take him eight long sums to work out the correct velocity for each of the hundreds of birds that, with luck, had returned that day from the race. Today the pigeon press advertises computers (£600 plus carriage) that do the job at the press of a button and then print out a list of members in order of velocity at the press of another button. Every club has a computer. The secretary is especially grateful for it when working out who's won the Average trophies and cups, because then he'll be dividing the total distances flown by each flyer's whole kit of birds by the total of their flying times – in sixtieths of yards and seconds.

When I started racing my birds I'd saved enough to buy my own clock, but a lot of men shared a clock then, hoping to win enough on the club pool for each to buy his own. The rules still allow for the time it takes a man who doesn't have the clock at his own loft to get to the other chap's loft where the clock is, and it's still so many minutes per mile depending on whether the man walks or rides his bike, with no allowance whatever for the man driving a car. The clock is set and securely locked on marking-up night, along with every one else's – a whole table-load of clocks awaiting the attention of the club secretary who synchronises with the club's master timer and then locks and seals them with a special pair of pliers and a lead seal.

Flyers arrive with their basket of birds and put their clock on the clock-setting table. Another special piece of pigeon racing gear, the ringer, is clamped to the book-keeping table. It looks like a bird's claw and it stretches the race ring to slip over the pigeon's claw and leave it on its leg at the pull and thrust of a handle. It doesn't take a couple of seconds. As each bird is taken from its basket and ringed the official calls out the number of the race ring, which is written in a ledger beside the number of the RPRA ring that the bird has worn all its life and the sex and colour of the bird. The name of the club and its telephone number is stamped on the under-surface of the bird's wing, and then it's put into a crate to be loaded with all the other birds for the journey to the race point. It won't be seen or fondled again by its owner until it returns under its own steam, which the owner hopes and prays it will. The crate is sealed with three seals to avoid the danger, however unlikely, that someone will find a means of getting his bird released at a point closer to home than the race point. Then most fanciers take their synchronised, locked and sealed clocks and head down the yard to the pub. Drinking isn't my pleasure, but I'm quite happy being there with my glass of orange squash, even if everyone else is so merry that I don't look merry enough.

As we all stood there talking on marking-up nights the Queen's pigeons were looked at as critically – and as fondly – as everyone else's, and what was interesting to everyone was what the Queen saw in her birds. They knew it was the birds the Queen came to see when she visited her lofts in my garden – not Gladys and me. At any club the talk is of birds and racing. The race programme is firmly fixed in everyone's mind because the flyer is deciding which birds to send and planning his own programme for the races so as to have the best chance of winning over the season. You train young birds as a team, and from watching them together you divide them into two teams for the racing season: one team you'll probably send to a race one week, the other team the next. Then when they're yearlings they join the old birds in a bigger team playing in a bigger league, flying such distances that the hours of daylight may well run out on the journey. It must be a horrifying sight for the racing bird, the sun low in the sky and the loft still over the horizon. The flyer at home watches the same sun getting low and wonders where his birds are.

But the flyer knows beyond a shadow of a doubt that the bird can find its way home alone without the assistance of a route planned by the AA. If the bird doesn't get home the chances are it's come to grief – a young bird might well have fallen in with a flock of pigeons and gone wild, and you wish it luck, but if it's an old bird with a mate and two eggs waiting in the nest you can be sure the poor creature is trying its very best to get home. The bird doesn't know the eggs are only pot eggs: being an honest creature it can't fathom the tricks men play on it.

Just how the bird does it is a matter of long and sometimes heated debate amongst flyers. Pet theories are propounded like gospel truth, but proving them is difficult and the argument goes on until past closing time, to be resumed the next week, and the next. It's the wise fancier who only knows that no one knows how the birds do it. People with no end of letters after their names make up theories to account for it, but in the end they have all had to admit it's a mystery.

One popular theory is that the birds use the earth's magnetism for a guide, as if they were flying compasses. This is an old chestnut. Magnetic and electrical theories on homing were first dreamed up by Victorian flyers, by gaslight, and they've stayed popular for over 130 years without a shred of evidence to back them up, and with one experiment after another coming to nothing. Birds have been transported to a race point inside a Faradic cage, safe from the smallest magnetic influence that might tell them where they're going; home the bird flies. Magnets have been attached to a bird's head and tail and under its wings – magnets no problem. (A bit annoying, though, the bird must think.) One boffin has released birds right in the shadow of a huge wireless transmitter that's filling the air about with high-strength Radio 4, to be counted upon for scrambling the birds' navigational skills. Not a bit of it.

What about the rotation of the earth, then, a clever person asks – I'll bet the birds can measure it, in the balance canals of their ears. And a poor bird will be operated on to interfere with its balance canals (a disgusting practice, the name of science notwithstanding) – and still it flies home. It flies home if it's taken to the race point under anaesthetic. It even flies home after being rotated on a gramophone turntable the whole length of the journey to the race point. The most devious routes have been taken to race points to avoid the possibility of the pigeon remembering the way home again, but somehow home it gets, barring accidents.

Some say the birds navigate by the stars – but they only fly during the day. Others say they measure the angle of the sun in the sky, but that doesn't tell them about *where* they want to go. To top it all, some others say that it's extra-sensory perception, but that's agreed, I would have thought – it is certainly an extra sense a pigeon has that a man doesn't, and to call it extra-sensory perception is like calling the Queen's crown a hat. There's no getting away from the mystery of it. And should the scientists be so clever as to solve the mystery, it won't be through simple-minded and cruel experiments; they'll have to take up fancying pigeons first. What the fancier has undoubtedly done over thousands of years, since Noah sent out the dove to look for land and report back to the Ark, is to improve the homing sense in the birds by selective breeding.

For what it's worth, my own theory is that the bird reads the ether like a pattern that has meaning for it, a pattern a man is denied knowing, being earthbound and complicated – and being a man, not a pigeon nor even a dog, a cat or a salmon. Pigeons aren't alone in having a homing sense, but a man doesn't have it any more than he has a lizard's ability to grow back a limb that's been lost – and perhaps he's more likely to learn the lizard's secret than the pigeon's. Perhaps the pigeon's secret is locked in the planet, not in its cells.

Given a fine day with a tailwind the birds fly high, six hundred feet above the earth, invisible to the naked eye, their horizon a curve in the blue distance. A headwind will bring them lower – they get beneath a headwind to swoop through valleys between the hills, low above trees, skimming moorland, just a yard above the heather on the fells, lifting at speed over dry stone walls and down again, a pack of them rippling over the walls. Within the first fifty miles of the race the thousands that were liberated together will divide into packs of two hundred or so birds that share a cruising speed, and for the first several hundred miles of the journey they share a destination – they're filled with a common purpose, and their cruising speed goes into overdrive as they carry each other along. In bad weather it's harder to stay together and the pack will be fragmented, flying low again, low enough to see ahead just a few yards, as though navigating by sight every inch of the way – which can't possibly be the case: the landscape is utterly strange, often foreign, to most of the birds. So the mystery deepens as it's probed . . . as through a glass darkly.

Another tantalising aspect is that training a bird over the last thirty miles to the loft makes a big difference to its chances of reaching home. Together with the selective breeding a fancier uses to get the best from his birds' natural gifts, training plays an important part in getting the birds to fly back to the loft. An untrained bird *can* get home again, but a trained bird jolly well *should*. There's obviously brain enough in that small feathered head to recognise landmarks for miles around the loft. Pressing hard for home with a pack of birds from the race point, flying with them hundreds of miles, a bird must decide when to peel off from the pack and make its way alone the last miles to the loft. You train a bird to make that crucial decision, and after five hundred miles in the free air the bird will zoom into a space six foot by six and stay there – exhausted.

I fly the open door method: in other words, I keep the loft open on race day so that the birds can dive unimpeded straight into their nest box, where I'm waiting with the clock, without wasting time negotiating a trap, when they would first have to pitch on to the trap board or even the roof of the loft. The birds have to be thoroughly tame for this method, because of course they can fly out again as easily as they flew in. However, if they are tame the flyer can count on them being tired enough to sit quietly until he picks them up to remove the race ring and put it into the thimble that fits into the clock. Then, with a satisfying sound, the time of the bird's arrival is recorded on a tape.

Pigeon men are the same now as when I started, for all it's a different world they live in – after all, the racing pigeon hasn't changed so that you would notice, or if it has changed it's only to become a better travelled, higher-mettled racer even than it was before.

In the days when trains took the birds to liberation points it seemed I was never on a station platform but there would be a stack of baskets with birds in them waiting to be loaded. Pigeon Specials were laid on, big express trains with eighteen wagons full of pigeons behind them. They might be going to France, Weymouth, Berwick or any one of dozens of race points all over the country, shunting out of sidings, snaking through the night. Pigeon traffic was such good business for the railways that they obliged with late starting times for the trains to suit the sport's officials rather than the timetable of their working hours. All the vans had to be moved from half a dozen local stations to meet up where the express was waiting for them – the organisation that went into it was marvellous, and that included loading the birds on and off trains and a Channel steamer should they be going to Dol, Vitré, Nantes, Marennes, Pau, Barcelona or San Sebastian. Nowadays it's a simple business driving a lorry on and off a ferry. It's not uncommon for a bird to fly the Channel a dozen or more times in its racing life; there was one Grooters cock from Leeds, a red pied, that flew it twenty-four times in eight years, and that was going by rail each time.

It was the rail strike in 1966 that finally did for the special relationship that had existed from the beginning between pigeon racing and trains. Some road hauliers were not slow to fill the gap, and because transport has to be organised on a grand scale if it's to be affordable at all, with Federations of flying clubs (which go by county or parts of a county, as a rule) laying on transport, or Combines (which are combined Federations, covering whole sections of the country) doing it, you can't have half the birds going by rail and half by lorry. So when British Rail decided it wasn't interested in carrying birds any more it was natural for the whole of the flying world to take to the roads – natural but sad, to my mind, for I love trains. Two things I'm glad about, that I was born in an age when horses were still used on the land, and that I was born such a long time before Mr Beeching got his hands on the railway network, so that I had a good long run of steam trains and branch lines to ride on.

These days a convoyer is sent with the birds on the lorry, to see to the birds' needs on a long trip, and to judge the suitability of the weather at the time scheduled for liberation. He will be on the telephone to the weather stations with whom the Federation has an agreement for the supply of up-to-date weather information along the route the birds will be taking. Birds have been kept for days in the lorries because of bad reports during those moments before the race is due to start. The convoyer keeps putting it off, afraid of a smash – and rightly so.

If the reports are good the sides of the lorries are opened by the driving crews. Pigeon transporters have sides that can be lowered, and all the baskets are revealed and the birds stir with the sudden fresh air, anticipating the journey. When the time comes, the sides of all the baskets in a row are opened together at the pull of a string, the bottom ones first, then tier by tier to the top. If the whole lot were opened together, from top to bottom, there would be carnage from the down-draught caused by the beating wings of the birds in the upper tiers, knocking the birds from below down onto the ground. The liberation is violent enough as it is with the controlled opening of the tiers of panniers; each pull of the string that opens them brings forth an ear-shattering explosion of feathers in flight. The sky darkens from the number of wings in the air, and the turbulence from the beating of all those wings together rocks a man nearly off his feet. There's wave upon wave of the birds lifting upwards, seeming to take the air you're breathing with them, sucking it upwards, a great spiral of birds, a swarm of them. They circle once, then they're gone. Before the dust has settled on the ground where you stand not a pigeon remains visible in the sky of all the thousands that filled it half a minute before. They've set course for home.

A smash is what the flyer dreads most. A single Federation's lorry might contain five thousand birds – if they're sent off when there's bad weather due they will be scattered, some to straggle home days later mud-soaked and hungry, some drifting in weeks later having been Lord knows where, a great many lost to the elements like so many bundles of feathers tossed away. People say for months afterwards, 'They never should have been liberated. The man should lose his job.' But it happens. Most often it's no one's fault, only fate.

When the season is over the prizes and the pool money are handed out at a grand dinner for the flyers. I didn't take part in the pool, and the birds were in the Queen's name and therefore the cash prizes were the Queen's cash, which I would send to Sandringham – just as the Queen paid the race money for every bird that was sent away during the season. But the cups I kept myself. In the early days I won so much it seemed like I couldn't lose, or rather that the Queen's birds couldn't lose. But I had casualties like everyone else. Every year some birds are lost from a loft, and as the wine flows at a flyers' dinner there comes a time for lamenting the beautiful lost birds of the season; then I feel as maudlin as the rest of them, for all that I'm still on orange squash.

A thunderstorm did for my favourite blue bar cock once, No. 63. It was the last race of the season, and I'd had my doubts about sending the bird for fear it might get lost since I wanted to breed from it. I witnessed the thunderstorm from inside a railway carriage where I was sitting with Gladys and her friend Mabel Hickson at Lynn Station – I was seeing them off on holiday, the only time in all our married life Gladys and I did not go on holiday together. I didn't want to go. Gladys wanted to go to Oberammergau for the Passion Play, and I was under the misapprehension that the play went on every day for a week and said that I didn't fancy that. The play did go on for a week, but it started Monday morning, finished Monday night, started Tuesday morning and so on. Sitting in the train I wished I was going. Beyond the window was lightning splitting the sky open, bucketing rain fit to drown a duck and thunder like the end of the world. No. 63 was out in it, as well as four other birds I would hate to lose. I knew they must be close to home by now, in the thick of it, and if it had been me going with Gladys instead of Mabel Hickson then all the birds would be safely tucked up in the lofts. Gladys and Mabel had a wonderful time. All the hotels were full, so they were put with a farmer and they lived like fighting cocks. Back in Lynn four out of the five birds got home, I'm glad to say – but not No. 63. He was sacrificed to the storm and my foolishness in not going to Oberammergau.

It's a sad gathering at the Swan on the day of a smash. The rules state that a flyer must deliver his clock to the club secretary for checking with the master timer within two hours of his first bird's arrival home, otherwise he will be penalised with so many minutes added to his bird's flying time. On the day of a smash the secretary sits waiting in the Swan yard. From around seven-thirty, when flyers would as a rule be breezing in with their clocks – and inside the clocks, their birds' race rings – some men drift in empty-handed, leaving someone at home to scan the horizon for the storm-battered birds. No news. They go home again, trying to conjure the birds out of thin air with the strength of their staring at the sky. Darkness falls like the hand of death on the loft, the empty perches and the decimated teams, and then the miserable flyers gather at the Swan to compare notes.

I would write to the Queen through Major Fellowes to tell her about her birds' successes. First I would get a letter of congratulation from Major Fellowes, then one from the Queen, most often dictated to her secretary, although I have had letters written in her very own hand, which I treasure the most. The losses I didn't write about. No matter how involved the Queen was with her birds she didn't live with them every day. The heartbreak was all mine. A mate of mine said to me, 'Len, never make a favourite of a pigeon, because you'll lose it.' But you can't help it, you still do.

I I

When I was a Carpenter

Once I was connected with the royal estate Gladys and I were invited every year to Sandringham for the party that was held for the farmers and tenants. In fact because of the numbers, there were two parties, about a hundred people going one night and another hundred the next. The Queen and whichever members of the family were staying at Sandringham would sit chatting with everyone for a couple of hours. It used to be held in the long library, which was a very beautiful room for a party, easy to sit down in and talk to people. Major Fellowes would be there, and Mr Pillar sometimes, but of course to start with I didn't know many of the other people apart from the Queen herself and Prince Philip. The Prince was always as nice as pie. He's a bloke who calls a spade a spade and it was always grand to meet him.

Gladys wasn't a big talker. She was content to sit quietly with an orange juice and enjoy the occasion, and she always looked nice. I was more of a mixer. There were all sorts of people in the long library whom I'd never come across before. I remember there was one man who asked me who I was so I told him – I thought by looking at him he was a working man, for he had a rugged face and was swarthy, with a ginger moustache. But when we shook hands I could tell that he hadn't worked with them, not ever. He was a lord. There were other people I thought must be lord this or lady that, but they weren't anything of the sort. But everywhere is like that now. You can't tell the difference between people any more. You see young girls in town, teenagers, all dressed up like ladies so you'd think they never went to work. I like to see them. It was a great credit to some of the old people what they used to do, taking in washing and ironing. Their linen was spotless, white as the driven snow, just with a bar of soap and a washboard. But you could tell they were washerwomen, and you could tell their daughters were the daughters of washerwomen, just by looking at them.

When Prince Charles was at Cambridge the Queen and Prince Philip made a home he could use for himself on the Wolferton Marsh and that *was* a home, an ordinary farmhouse on the estate. The Queen once told me she loved Wood Farm better even than Sandringham because it was so peaceful and secluded, with woods all around. It was hard for an ordinary chap to conceive of living at Sandringham – the grandeur of it, the quality, how well maintained everything was, with a staff of God knows how many doing shifts to wait on you hand and foot. What must it be like, I used to wonder, to be waited on hand and foot? As if there was no excuse for the people of the house to wear out as they grew old any more than the chandeliers did.

When I got that letter from Major Fellowes asking me to go to Sandringham to talk to him, I thought I would be going there to do some joinery work, which I would have been happy to do. The jobs I loved most were restoring old mouldings, skirting boards and staircases. I loved matching two pieces of wood so no one could tell they hadn't grown together on the same tree, and I was always keen for jobs that meant using the old hand tools to repair a piece of work, so that the lines of it got back their beauty.

It had taken me a very long time to set up in business as a carpenter for myself. Until after the Second World War I was a tradesman, working by the hour – and with an hour's notice (to clean up my tools) if the job was coming to a close. I stayed two years 'improving' at Billy Hill's, but by then Mr Hill had become very friendly with a butcher named Sutherland. When a butchering business came on the market out in the village of Gayton, that was the end of Billy Hill the builder – he became a butcher. But he found two chances for me when he gave up his building business. One was in the shop, doing bench work for 10d an hour, for J. J. Bone, and the other was with Teddy Nape at a shilling an hour, but always on the building. I chose the 10d an hour job because I wanted to be on the bench.

I chose the right one, because when I went to Bone's there was a chap there named Charlie White who was, I should think, the most brilliant craftsman in King's Lynn. There was another lad who had been an apprentice there, but I think he'd wasted his opportunity and Charlie had got a bit fed up with him. As a result Charlie cast all his favours on me, and I owe all I know of bench work to him. I worked with Charlie on the most beautiful pitch pine staircase in the YMCA, which is still there. I would have stayed working at Bone's, but I was laid off. The first time I was laid off I got so fed up looking for a local job I went to Lynn Station one Saturday morning to get on a train down to Hertfordshire, where I heard there was work. I was standing on the platform when one of Bone's men came for me to say Bone had another job.

But I was laid off again, and it wasn't so easy to think of going away because Gladys and I had just got married – I was out of work for a year. It was 1936, so I wasn't alone – there were queues of us down the labour exchange, reporting nearly every day, and at the end of the week they would hand out 25s, which they wouldn't if you hadn't signed on day after day. One morning someone might be missing from the queue and you got right narked to think he'd got a job and you hadn't, of all the daft things.

I would cycle round the villages looking for work, and I tried all the builders in the town. I got so that I hoped and prayed to God that a man would say no when I asked for a job. Then one day I went to a man named Ives. One of four brothers, he was one of the best builders in Lynn, and he did a tremendous lot of railway work because his brother-in-law was one of the inspectors in the railway works department. I knocked on the door, saying to myself I hoped he would turn me down. Ives opened the door, and he was a huge fellow with a moustache and glasses and a gruff voice. 'What do you want?' he shouted. What a way to speak to anybody!

I said, 'I wondered if you've got the chance of a job for me?'

'What are you?'

'A carpenter,' I told him.

He said, 'Hmph!' Then he said, 'Yes.'

I said I'd been more or less used to shop work, but he didn't let me finish.

'Bring your tools up in the morning,' he shouted, and slammed the door.

I took my tools to his shop next morning only to find there were another five blokes, as well as me – grown men to what I was.

'You, you, you, you, you – on the lorry to Wolferton,' said Ives to the others. Then he pointed at me and said, 'You, up those steps to my brother. He's making a set of stairs up there.' His brother Gus was the one who did all the joinery work. He was the one who had the money, through his wife, but he was only a worker for his brother.

He was a nice fellow. He put me on a bench next to him and said, 'Round those noses up and shoot those risers.'

I'd done a stack of them when Ives came around about eleven o'clock. He didn't say anything, just ran his hand along one of the noses to see if it was nice and smooth. 'That's right, my lad,' he said. 'Build more like that.'

I went home to Gladys that night and I told her I wouldn't be there five minutes because of the other five blokes. At the end of the first week one got the sack. The next week another bloke got the sack. 'He'll sack me next, I'm sure he will,' I said to Gladys. But I survived the lot of them. He never sacked me at all, not for years.

The stairs I was working on were for the big hotel at Hunstanton Station. Ives was working on two stations then, Wolferton Station, which was the royal station for Sandringham, and Hunstanton. It was a tremendous hotel at Hunstanton. We did no end of work on it – not only all the joinery, but some of Ives's men put in a spiral staircase six storeys high as a fire escape – then after we'd done all that, it was pulled down. 'I'd rather it'd burned down,' said Elijah Hornigold, who was Ives's foreman carpenter. 'At least the fire escape would have been used.'

I worked at Wolferton Station as well. When I went into the royal waiting room to repair some of the doorjambs I walked towards the huge looking glass that was over the washbasins in the royal toilet. Much to my great surprise and fright, I suddenly started to descend. It was only three inches or so, but I wondered what was happening for a minute, until I heard a flushing noise in the toilets and realised that was how they worked. The concrete round those doorjambs there was the hardest I've had to chip away in my whole career: it was like iron.

I worked for Ives right up to the war. The week before war was declared he laid me off, then a week later he sent for me again to help blackout Hillington Hall for the troops. That was the huge hall where Lord and Lady Downe lived – Lord Downe was a prominent Reffley Brother. The soldiers ruined the lovely oak staircase and the floors with their hobnail boots. We made frames with one-by-two-inch wood for the blackout material to fit properly. At the chapel they had tried putting up curtains to blackout the windows, but it was a failure. I was at a men's meeting there one night and the warden came in to complain. Mr Pilling took care of him. Mr Pilling was one of the leading chapel members and he was the boss at Savage's, the big engineering firm at North End. He said he would send for me if anything cropped up. I came home from working at Hillington Hall one evening and Gladys said, 'Mr Pilling sent for you, Len.' So I went and told Ives.

'Don't worry, my lad,' shouted Ives. 'You go. You'll get a job there for the whole of the war. I don't mind you going. I don't want to hold you back.'

And so I did.

12

The War Comes to Lynn

Gladys and I were in chapel on the Sunday morning war was declared. I'd already joined the Special Police and everyone was supposed to be ready for the announcement, but when the news actually came everyone was so upset that the service couldn't go on. We went home and I started making shutters for the windows straightaway: I thought the bombs were going to be falling any minute. At a quarter to three on the Monday morning we were catapulted out of bed by a siren going off. We threw on some clothes and rushed out into the street, but nothing happened – no sleep happened after that, either. On the Wednesday morning I was down in the lofts, when the siren went again – Gladys told me it went off just as her feet touched the floor when she was getting out of bed to start the day, and she was unsettled all day as though she'd swallowed a live eel. By day the weather continued lovely and sunny and right hot, but everything was upside down and it was so dark at night.

We had two evacuee girls, about thirteen years old, to live with us. There were crowds and crowds of children and their mothers arriving in Lynn from London the weekend the war started. Being headmistress of the school a lot of them would be going to, Flossie was made responsible for seeing that the children had billets. She worked from morning till midnight – some of them were real waifs and strays and she had a terrible time placing them. Our two were quite nice, for a couple of days, but they were soon crazy to go home again to Bethnal Green, and they were cheeky as anything. They wouldn't budge from the house to go to chapel or Sunday school. We would've had to drag them there kicking and screaming to get them to go – to get them to go anywhere with us. They got naughtier every week, and it was impossible to imagine just where it might end. Then one Sunday around Christmas their mothers came and took them away by train, and we never saw nor heard from them again.

At Savage's we were making portable aeroplane hangars that were all being sent to somewhere near Oxford and from there to France. Great dome-shaped things they were, all in sections, and all made of hardwod – elm and oak. I should think it took every single bit of hardwood growing in Norfolk. It was a wonderful job, and I had a good mate to work with. We weren't allowed to use anything like a mechanical screwdriver – it all had to be done by hand so that each screw we put in was really doing what it was supposed to do, and not being forced through the wood. But then the Germans marched all the way through Belgium and France and that put an end to that job.

I fell back on blackout work – I blacked out the whole of Gaywood Hall from end to end, on my own. When Lord Bagge died the Lynn Corporation had bought the Hall and two surgeons, Mr Lewin and Mr Harrison, leased it from them as a high-class nursing home. Since I'd worked for Bone I'd done jobs on my own account in the evenings, bookcases and desks, and I'd worked for both the surgeons at their private homes, so when they took on the Hall it was natural for me to work for them there. One morning Lord Fermoy, Princess Diana's grandfather, came up there with Lady Fermoy. He was ill, and he remained in the Hall and died there. I knew Lord Fermoy because he was President of the King's Lynn Football Club, and I had seen Lady Fermoy with him several times. I stopped her one morning when she came up to see Lord

Fermoy at the Hall and I asked her how His Lordship was. She was so upset and worried she could only tell me how poorly he was. But, after Lord Fermoy died, every time I saw her in the street Lady Fermoy would stop and say hello. She promised to come and see me at home no end of times, but that was because she was so polite, and such a lovely lady.

I'd soon done more than my share of blackout work in Lynn and there wasn't a window left in the town that hadn't been made safe against the night. I was out of work again. My father, now retired, took care of a rich old man's lawn from time to time – the old man's name was a household word in Lynn for decorating and plumbing. William Lock had a huge number of painters and plumbers working for him, and he did all the work at Sandringham, including making all the royal coffins. Lock would go himself to Sandringham every working day to keep up with what needed doing there. One of his plumbers, Len Plane, was always given the job of lining the coffins in lead. There are vaults up at Gaywood Hall where the Bagges are at rest, and their coffins were made by Lock's carpenters and lined in lead by Len Plane. One day my father told old man Lock that I was out of a job.

'Tell that boy to take his tools along down the Wootton Road there. I'll give him a fortnight's work,' said Lock.

So I went there and made a start. During the morning the boss, Percy Dockerell, came round. Dockerell was the builder and Lock was the man who provided the money. Before that Dockerell was a carpenter working for a firm in Lynn, just like me, but then he started on his own and he built all the posher houses up the hill towards Gayton, under contract to old man Lock.

'I see you made a start, then,' said Dockerell. He was just back from London with all the architect's plans he would use. 'Any rate, I must say you look like a tradesman,' he said to me, 'which is more than my two at the shop do. You'd think they worked in a bank.'

I was wearing brown overalls. I always wore brown overalls. I knew the joiners he had working for him because I had been an apprentice with one of them at Billy Hill's. They were two extremely good joiners, but they always went to work in their Sunday suits. One of them would never push a barrow up the street because he was courting a schoolteacher and trying to impress her.

'You know how long I can keep you, don't you?' said Dockerell. 'No longer than a fortnight.' The house I was working on was all but finished.

'I'll stay as long as you like,' I said, and he replied, 'No doubt you will,' and that fortnight became nine years. I only left working for Dockerell to set up on my own.

Eventually the war did reach Lynn. I'd been doing duty as a lookout for nearly three years, and after spending all that time sitting on top of St Margaret's church looking for planes in an empty sky I now found myself staring night after night at what seemed to be the whole of the Luftwaffe droning over Lynn on its way to bomb Sheffield, or Coventry, or Lynn itself. Although I was right on top of the church tower I was covered from head to foot in mud once, from a bomb dropping into the river right next to it. My job was to telephone information down to the station, but you couldn't count the planes – they just kept coming. Until then the most exciting thing that had happened while I was lookout was when Princess Margaret came to the church for a special service. It was dark as anything with the blackout, and the Inspector turned to me and said, 'Stand there, boy, and open the gate for her. As soon as she comes in, shut the gate,' which I did.

The first bombs that fell on this part of the world came down just along the road from us – Gladys and I dived under the bed. There was no let-up after that, but we never got under the bed again when we heard the planes coming; we decided it was safer outdoors. So when the whole of the length of the Gayton Road was machine-gunned by enemy planes Gladys and I were lying outside in the potato rows less than a hundred yards from the road. The planes seemed as though they were right overhead and low enough to touch – with one mind Gladys and I scuttled the shortest distance across the vegetable patch to the side door of the house, driven by terror, which struck me as a feeling even beetles and worms probably feel, like an instinct, at the approach of a predator.

Coming away from visiting Steele at his house at Sandringham I would hear the bombs falling in the distance. On nights when I didn't have my bike I would catch the bus home. Waiting at the bus stop I would suddenly hear the pheasants cackling. The next thing there would be searchlights going all over the sky, then the bombs – the pheasants always heard the planes coming before a man could hear them. The Sunday school building of our Tower Street chapel was turned into a mortuary for the war. At first it seemed that it would stay empty, but not any more. When Lynn was bombed chains of us would be pulling bricks away all night. When St John's Terrace came down, we were still pulling the bricks away around five or six in the morning, and we found the bed linen under a cupboard that was smashed in little pieces. There was blood all over it, or so we thought – but it wasn't blood at all, it was jars of jam. The two old ladies that lived there were in the cellar, suffocated: when they were found at about eleven in the morning they weren't touched, just dead.

One afternoon in the summertime there was a dominoes and darts match at the Eagle Hotel in the centre of the town, the RAF chaps against the local chaps, with a tea laid on. That hotel suffered a direct hit in the worst tragedy of the war in Lynn. Forty people were killed, nine of them so completely blown apart there was nothing you could identify to take to the mortuary in Tower Street.

King's Lynn was full of airmen, brought into the town in lorries every night. You noticed the Americans most. Gladys had given up working at Donaldson's when we got married, but after the two girls from Bethnal Green went home she went back to work there for the rest of the war. Mrs Donaldson was running the business while her husband was in the RAF at Preston. Gladys didn't like Mr Donaldson, but the wife was a wonderful woman – I should say the best-looking woman in King's Lynn. All the Americans fell for her. On Tuesday nights she would give parties for them in the room above the shop. When Mr Donaldson came home on leave he didn't like what was going on at all, especially the fact that Mrs Donaldson was more successful at running the shop than he ever was. Somehow or other he got out of the RAF and came home, but Gladys carried on working there because Mrs Donaldson pleaded with her to stay.

We never went hungry, right through the war and right through rationing, because Mrs Donaldson made sure we got pheasant and partridge and any amount of fish. She would have given Gladys her very last bit of game in the shop. And it was through Mrs Donaldson that I was able to start in business on my own. Out the back of the shop was the big old room where the ice used to be made – where I took my thumb when I planed the end off it when Gladys was a girl – and it was part of an old building that had been a pub. Mrs Donaldson let me have one side of it for five bob a week – 'Just to keep the books straight,' she said.

The war was a quiet time for me with my birds because racing had been suspended and training wasn't allowed except for birds on active service. All I could do was supply the forces with young birds, as most pigeon fanciers did, free. Some two hundred thousand young birds were given to the Services by British fanciers so they could be trained for use in military lofts. Thousand upon thousand of them were dropped one by one by parachute over enemy territory in Europe, with instructions and a questionnaire for the finders. Nine out of ten birds were never heard from again – they fell into enemy hands or cooking pots, or came to grief crossing the Channel –

but the birds that did get back carried information that could never have been obtained any other way.

Steele had won pigeon racing cups for King George VI as Royal Lofts manager, but the only honour he displayed on the wall of his front room was the Dickin Medal that one of the King's birds was awarded in the war. The Dickin Medal is the highest award for animals and birds on war service, like an animal VC. Only fifty-two of them were awarded through the whole of the war, and of these pigeons received thirty-one.

The royal birds had been carried by RAF planes flying out of Norfolk on bombing missions. They were to be used for emergency communications in the event of a forced landing, and the royal bird that was awarded the Dickin Medal, a blue cock named Royal Blue, was the first pigeon of the war to bring home a message from a crew in distress. By the time it reached the lofts at West Newton the crew were in enemy hands in Holland, but their position and condition were known and I imagine the colleagues and families of the men were hugely relieved to know they were alive.

Some birds flew an astonishing number of missions with bomber crews, and if they were very lucky they would return safely in the bosom of the plane to England. One bird bred and trained by a Nottingham flyer had been on over one hundred operational bomber sorties, and it homed from diverted or force-landed planes several times with details of the plight of the air crews. Then it was thought lost along with the plane it had been in over Cologne on a bombing raid there in 1943. Nearly three weeks later it staggered into its loft. Its breastbone had been broken and its flight feathers were mangled, but it had got home over all those hundreds of miles of war-torn land. Other birds reached their lofts only to drop dead from injuries that should have killed them before they'd flown the great distance they had to cover to get there – to die. The Dickin Medal returned to the possession of the Royal Family on Steele's death and we all hoped there would never be cause for pigeons to win medals in war in the future.

13

Independence

The war was over, thank God, but you still needed a licence to get timber and materials if you wanted to work for yourself. I had wanted to do so for years, and now I was going to. I knew my father thought I was mad, but then he had always thought I was a time waster, with all the football I'd played and the hours and hours I would spend talking with birds that didn't even lay eggs a man could eat. The President of King's Lynn Football Club at that time was Lord Wise, and he got my licence for me. I came home one day from the Arsenal with Gladys after watching England play the Russian Dynamos there, and my licence was in the front door.

I wanted to be independent, to come and go as I liked. When I was working for a boss I would work every night for myself, in a garage. Whenever I went off on Saturday mornings to get to a football match, I would work overtime of an evening to make up for it, not wanting to embarrass my boss. But work was what I did to provide the wherewithal for doing what really mattered to me – it was never an end in itself, as I believe it was for my father. It was true what he said, that I wasted hours and hours, years of my life, enjoying myself – 'It's a good thing not everyone is like you,' he would say. And he was convinced I would come a cropper, setting up on my own.

Not long after I got my licence I was doing a garage in the middle of the town, fitting it out with tool racks and a workbench. I was still in the Special Police, and one day when I popped into the station during my lunch break who should come in the back door but old Frank Crisp from Lowestoft. I'd known him when he was a player for Lowestoft and he played against the Lynn team, and he'd just moved to Lynn to take charge as the building inspector for the town. A new police station was going to be built.

'What are you doing, then?' he asked.

I told him.

'Well, what about coming and working for me on the police station?'

'I don't mind,' I said, and I was with him till he died, thirty years later.

The old station, where we had reported during the war, was a cramped old stone building of the same vintage as the library across the road; but whereas the library is imposing and lofty, in the same rusty-coloured stone that Sandringham is built of, that goes a nice dull red with age, the police station was dark and flinty to look at and the walls were too thick for its size. The new station was to be modern and spacious, in brick, with columns of brick outside as simple and straight as an honest man. Everyone agreed it was an improvement, and there was a huge amount of joinery that had to be done inside. The lost property office, for instance: we fitted out one room with a counter and some shelves, but within a month of the station being in use it was obvious the room wasn't half big enough, so we had to fit out another room with shelves from floor to ceiling round three sides. You would have been surprised to see what was lost in the normal course of a day in Lynn: tractor tyres, pushchairs, even flower-pots. But all the rooms needed shelves in them for paper, finger-printing equipment, helmets and so on. There was the front counter that swung up and open, and benches in the cells for the prisoners to sleep on. I was always being called back to the cells to fix the doors because the locks had gone wrong – the claustrophobia put the wind up me. There was a bell to ring if you got locked in – but you didn't know if the bell was working or not. You didn't hear anything – it just showed up as a red light in the office.

Once the police station was built Fred kept me on for the general run of repairs there, and at the police houses and at all the council places, the schools and old people's homes. I loved the Grammar School and the High School, where Gladys went as a girl. But the school at Gaywood Park was a terrible place. The kids would smash things up while you were there, especially in the toilet places, pulling tiles off around the sink – and there I was, telling them not to, which made as much difference as telling the wind to stop blowing the tiles off a roof.

When the Donaldsons sold up the shop and the whole lot was pulled down I had to move my workshop, and I was lucky to get space in the grounds of Gaywood Hall. The council had taken over the Hall again and turned it into a college, which it is to this day, but the old farm buildings were still empty and thanks to Fred Crisp I was able to rent them. I kept four or five hundred chickens there as well, and some pigs.

From an early age I'd gone pig keeping for Mr Playford once the harvest had been gathered in. The pigs were turned out on to the stubble and I would stay with them right through the day, but it was tricky. Even getting them to the field was tricky. You had to take the little ones first so that their mothers followed peacefully, otherwise the old sows were sure you were trying to separate them from their piglets and they would turn on you. One particularly vicious sow would run at me with her mouth open to bite me if she was given the smallest opportunity of imagining I meant her babies harm. Keeping the pigs in the field once the pickings of stubble got slim was another headache – the next field looked greener to the pigs, and they were determined to get into it. I would have to head them off with a stick when they got to any space in the hedge they could barge through. Once I didn't have the stick in my hand because I'd been too busy at the blackberries growing in a clump in the corner of the field and had lost it there. I reached the gap in the hedge before the pigs did, but the vicious old sow wasn't stopping for a little boy who weighed just a fraction of what she weighed – I was tossed away like so much straw, head over heels, and the sow got started on the beets in the next field, with all her mates following at a trot behind her.

I thought that was the end of my pig keeping days, but Mr Playford's sense of humour saved me. I thought the same thing again when one of the old sows ran off as we arrived at a field up the lane in the opposite direction to the farm – it would have taken a steam roller to stop her. I followed her for more than a mile, running like mad, but she disappeared and I lost her. When we got back to the farmyard around four in the afternoon to my surprise the sow was already there, lying up to her chin in her filthy straw and taking a good rest.

In those days I wasn't nearly as fond of pigs as my father was, but when I had the chance to keep them myself I found loving pigs was in my blood after all. I bought a couple of beauties from my cousin in West Lynn. My father was a very frail old man by then but he would boil up all the swill for them. I went around town with my hand barrow collecting scraps from all the food and vegetable shops, and my father would boil it up in a copper. Poor old boy – I came up there one day and he'd been chopping wood for the copper and he'd toppled over. He couldn't get up again, and he died without ever using the wood he'd chopped. It was only after he died that I found out what he really thought about me. At his funeral every one of his friends came and told me how proud my father had been of me, how much he thought of me – how he would sing my praises to them. I'd never known that while he was alive. Not once had he said anything of the sort to my face, nor to Gladys.

A bloke from Hillington came and took my two pigs away

to the boar and brought them back. I fed them up and they got bigger and bigger. I was looking forward to the piglets, but local vandalism was terrible by then. After the war more of the Gaywood Hall estate had been given over to a new council estate, and London got rid of thousands and thousands of people to it. They must have been some of the worst in London, to judge from the destruction that went on all around. Every weekend their relations came by train to visit them. I had put up corrugated iron fencing eight feet tall around the pigs and chickens but that didn't keep the lads from the estate out – they pulled it down. So I had to pack my chickens up. I sold the sows while they were still in pig, and I never went in for pigs again.

There was never any of that sort of thing when I was a boy. In King's Lynn itself there were only about four to six celebrities who were wrong 'uns, but they were a bit tenpence to the shilling, as the saying is. There were Inkerman Lake, Quiver Goodson and Ginger Wilkin, and a few others – the police knew their names. One or other of them would throw a brick through a window to get in the lock-up for Christmas so they would get a good dinner – things like that. When some crime or other was committed, the police knew where to go, or at least where to start looking. And when dealing with the kids the policemen would clip their ears and give them a good telling off, and that would be the end of it.

The Reffley Temple survived the war intact but not the peacetime that came after. The woods are still there, to a smaller degree, and the spring still splashes into the big bowl beneath the monument. The water is amazingly hard. It was the same water as came out of the big old pump in the Playford farmhouse, and I remember when I was a boy I left a glass half full of water on a windowsill there. The glass just stood there for about a fortnight and the hardness of the iron in the water cut it right through – the glass broke clean in half at the level of the water that was left in it. But the vandals came with the peace, ransacked the Temple, smashed up the huge, beautiful table and the pictures on the walls and made off with the silverware. The silver was found later in the woods, but of course it wasn't put back in the Temple. The two stone lions were taken to Hillington Hall for safe keeping, and the weather got inside the old building and brought decay. I don't know what happened to the secret of the punch.

14

Good Companions

The very first time the Queen came to my house I had told her about a project I had under way that was to last four or five years: I'd made up my mind to visit every League football ground in Great Britain. There are ninety-two of them, but in the end I visited ninety-three because Queen's Park Rangers decided one year to play at the White City. Each year the Queen wanted to know which towns I had visited and how many more there were to be visited before I had the whole of League football under my belt. The Queen travels all over the world, but she can't go down to the railway station and buy a ticket to anywhere she fancies. She would have to take her own train if she wanted to zig-zag around the country like I did in pursuit of another League ground, and the whole of Fleet Street would be following, playing havoc with the railway timetables. I told the Queen I wouldn't have her job for a pension – 'That's an old Norfolk saying, Your Majesty,' I added, but I don't think she took me wrong, anyway.

While I was going all over the country fulfilling this mad ambition they got so used to seeing me down at the railway station in Lynn that the stationmaster started up a joke that I was trying to buy my own train, with all the money I spent there. When I paid over for my ticket, Harry in the booking office would say, 'That's another wheel you've bought today, Len.' It took just four years to visit all the grounds, in the end.

What did take some sticking was visiting the Fourth Division clubs of the north. They weren't as good as Lynn, some of them, and Lynn's never been a League club. So I persuaded Gladys to come with me.

We planned it most carefully, like a campaign. The most number of matches on consecutive days were over the Easter weekend. On the map we worked out we could get to Carlisle for the Good Friday match, on to Barrow for the Saturday match, Workington for Monday Bank Holiday for another match, and then there was a match on Tuesday in Bury. This took a number of trains and buses with some hairline scheduling, but we got off to a good start. What should we see just outside the station at Carlisle but an old fellow pushing a home-made barrow stacked with baskets of pigeons. He was having trouble pushing it and there was a bitterly cold wind, but with Gladys and me to help we got the pigeons to the old man's loft on his allotment. It was a lovely spot, and I stayed friends with the old fancier, Mr Ingram, for years afterwards.

Good Friday morning we found a Baptist church to go to, then we took a bus across the border into Scotland, just so we could say we'd been to Gretna Green, and of course in the afternoon we went to the match. To get to Barrow for the next day's match we took a bus over Shap Fell with the wind howling and snow falling – a very rough ride – to Kendal. From there we caught a connection to Barrow and straight to the football ground. The digs we found overlooking More-cambe Bay were not promising – there was a very young man in the house all on his own. But he was marvellous. 'Sunny Boy,' Gladys called him because he was so nice – and he cooked us some smashing meals. Almost next door was a Methodist chapel where we went for the Easter Sunday service – and the minister there looked familiar. He had preached at our Gaywood chapel while he was training. There were fanciers I knew in Barrow whom we went to see in the afternoon. It was a marvellous weekend because everyone was so friendly, and for the Monday match Gladys and I had a magnificent train ride right up the west coast to Workington, looking out over the sea the whole way with the sun shining. It was a good match – Workington beat Stockport 4–0. Not only that, we walked all along the docks there afterwards, and up the coast path beyond was a pigeon loft looking right out over the sea. The door was open and, a bit like a nosey pigeon, I walked in to talk to the fancier – he had some grand birds, living just like their forebears the old rock-doves.

We were back with Sunny Boy for another night before catching the first bus to Preston and then one to Bury for the match in the afternoon. Then we had the long train ride home. We were waiting for a Peterborough train until two in the morning on Manchester Station, both of us dazed and Gladys with a headache so bad I could almost feel it. So she surprised me by agreeing to come with me again in the autumn, to Birkenhead and Oldham, Halifax, Southport and Chester, and then the next Easter to Stockport, Rochdale and Preston. And so it went on. At Dartford we stayed in the same hotel as the whole of the Black and White Minstrel Show. We had some good runs. There was hardly a town where I didn't find a loft to look in on, even if I didn't know of one beforehand – there were still baskets of pigeons piled on the platforms in those days, to give a fancier a clue of where to go.

Then we got to the last ground to be visited, and it was Exeter. Gladys came with me because my mate Jack Savage had told someone he knew at the Exeter club what I had been up to over the last four years, and theirs was the final ground – they made a huge fuss over us. Gladys and I went to Plymouth the next day, to stay with the agent for the National Children's Homes who always used to stay with us when he was in Norfolk. I would go round Gaywood collecting money for him every Christmas time.

'You know who lives here, don't you?' I said to Gladys when we were in Plymouth. 'Eileen. Eileen and Tom.' I meant

Eileen Starr, and the fellow she'd married just before I married Gladys, Tom Harrington. They had moved away from Lynn and we hadn't seen them for thirty years.

We found the street they lived in and knocked on the door. Gladys had cured me of my infatuation with Eileen just as soon as I started going out with her, but you always remember so well the face of someone you idolised for a while. When the door was opened I thought it was Eileen's mother. I had a terrible shock when I realised it was Eileen. I was expecting to see her as she had been, when my own common sense should have told me that all her lovely black hair and Welsh beauty would be gone. She'd become the image of her own mother.

We kept in touch after that. About four years later Gladys and I were in Plymouth again, so we knocked on the door. There was no answer. We put a note through the door, and when we got home there was a note through *our* door, from Eileen and Tom. They had come to see us while we were in Plymouth hoping to see them, and that was the only time in all those years they had come to Lynn.

When my father died Gladys and I had been free to go on holiday for the first time since we were young – first my mother had been bad, then Gladys's mother, then my father, and now we were making up for lost time. So Gladys and I started going to different countries. We made a lot of friends that way, like we did when we were touring the League grounds. We'd meet a couple, then perhaps in four years' time we would meet them again on another tour. When I think how my parents never went anywhere in their whole lives for a holiday except to Yarmouth, always to the same boarding house five minutes from the sea, I was really spreading my wings.

We went to some fourteen or fifteen countries during those trips abroad. The tour I liked best was round Denmark, Norway and Sweden. I loved every mile of it – the work they do in wood there, the freshness of it, the green earth and the water, the fjords so fresh and crisp like they were new. Some places I didn't like. In France, you had to boil the water and the waiters were rude; in Italy Gladys was so ill she could hardly stand up when we got to Pisa to see the leaning tower.

· I think I must favour the north, the daylight there, because the other trips I loved most were to the islands off Scotland. I got to see Lerwick, where some of my birds have won from. When we went to the race point I felt like abandoning the tour so that we could stay to see the trucks arrive on the Saturday morning. I could picture them there on the grass, parked in a long line, truck after truck filled with birds anxious to get home again when they'd hardly arrived. It would be early morning, the time I love most of all, with the light streaming from the east, a gentle mist rising off the sea and dew on the grass. The birds would have to be released very first thing to give them the chance of reaching home the same day.

Going to Belgium is exciting for any pigeon man because the sport is everywhere there. They have brick lofts and stone lofts, lofts on their roofs, a lot of them ramshackle family lofts – but the birds are spectacular. For all the way their lofts look, the fanciers in Belgium make most Englishmen feel like beginners no matter how long they've been keeping birds. I told the Queen about my visit to Belgium, and I explained that one of the differences was that the Belgians don't keep any but the best birds so they only have forty or fifty racers, usually widowhood cocks, in their lofts, no matter how prominent the lofts might be.

The Queen had got to know a great many birds in the Royal Lofts and she would recognise them each year when she came to visit, though it was difficult keeping up with each crop of young birds year after year. But she still couldn't see that it would be a good idea to pare down the number of the birds to so few, and I was glad she felt that way.

'You have to be with them every day from when they're hatched to know them all, Your Majesty,' I said, and having just been to Belgium I explained a new practice I had seen there. 'Now I don't hold no brief for the foreigner,' I said, 'but in this I think they're very good. We always, from time immemorial, had an aluminium ring for the bird. These days the foreigner has coloured aluminium rings, a different colour for each year, so you can tell at a glance which year the bird was born in, which makes it a lot easier to pick out one from another.' She agreed it was a good idea, but it hasn't happened yet, not in this country.

Another country I didn't go to, and which Gladys didn't go to either, entirely through my fault, was Yugoslavia. Gladys had arranged everything. We got an early train to London because we were going to a match at Wembley in the afternoon and leaving on the evening train. When we got to Victoria Station after the match there were various parties standing on the platform, but none of them was going to Yugoslavia. We waited and waited until I went and made some enquiries, leaving Gladys with the luggage, and it seemed the party we were waiting for had left that morning. The twenty-four-hour clock had just been introduced and I had mistaken the time. So Gladys and I went home again.

My friend Jack Savage said, 'I wouldn't be unduly worried, Len. I'd go to Llandudno,' which we did, and we had a lovely time. We met some lovely people at the chapel there.

The Queen knew that Gladys and I were involved with the chapel. I told her how my parents had been Primitive Methodists – the poor relations, if you like – and the Methodists were the richer people. When I joined Tower Street chapel, where I met Gladys, I moved out of the Primitive Methodists into the Methodists, just before the two of them got together around 1930.

Gladys was so committed to the chapel that she became a lay preacher herself. She took a correspondence course to qualify, but that was very hard. The first year the Queen came to see us, Gladys was working on her passing-out sermon, which she gave at Clenchwarton, and the Queen had been very encouraging when Gladys told her about it. But she ought to have taken the correspondence course years before, when she was a young woman. She put too much into her sermons. I go to church now, since the Methodists in Gaywood have merged with the church, and the sermons don't last above ten minutes. Gladys's used to go on for ages and ages. I would tell her she put too much into them but it didn't make any difference, she was dedicated to it. She would spend the whole week working on what she would say when Sunday came along, then she would go to one chapel in the afternoon and another in the evening, and read out her sermon.

The Queen was always very interested in how Gladys was getting on with her preaching, and Gladys would tell her she was enjoying it, but she had the most terrible nerves beforehand. The Queen sympathised, and that gave Gladys strength. There was so much she wanted to say, not so much about the Bible but about telling the truth, learning to trust, the inner light in people, doing the work of God, loving thy neighbour: everything that was difficult to say. Gladys had tremendous faith, and what she liked best was to listen to an old-fashioned sermon from the heart. Having been driven to become a local preacher by her faith she gave her best, but she never stopped being shy. That was why Gladys liked the Queen so much. The first time she met the Queen, Gladys said to me afterwards, 'Len, she's so nice, there's no need to be afraid of her at all.' And from then on Gladys was always at home with the Queen.

15

Losses

Both Gladys and her sister Flossie loved sport – it was one of the things that brought us together and kept us together. Flossie kept up her season ticket at the Walks ground for years, and used to go there with her friend Kate Bouty. Flossie and Gladys both liked to watch sport on television – Gladys especially loved the boxing – and often Gladys would be at home with Flossie in the evenings watching the television while I was out, or they would be practising for a recital that the King's Lynn Musical Society was going to give. Gladys would play the piano and Flossie would sing. These were the evenings I liked most to be home, and Gladys would play hymns for me because she knew how much I loved them. Most popular songs don't last, but hymns and carols go on for ever. I hate it when the hymnbooks keep being changed and old hymns left out, which the Methodists do. I can't forgive that. In our Sunday school days we had the *Sunday School Hymn Book* and it contained some marvellous hymns, like 'If I were a beautiful twinkling star I'd shine with all my might.' There were loads of lovely hymns the children would sing the way they were meant to be sung. You don't find hymns like that in the hymnbooks today, but then you don't find the kids going to Sunday school as they once did, either.

One day Gladys said to me, 'I think Flossie knows she's going to die.' Flossie had all of a sudden started giving me cheques for different things, saying things like, 'Buy that ladder you want, Len.' She'd never once given me money before, although she'd had a good job all her life and she'd never had to pay rent or buy a house. She'd always given me a good present for Christmas and for my birthday, and she was always buying me books, but she'd never given me money before. She would stay with us every Christmas right to the New Year, and when Mrs Towler was dying the poor old girl lived with us for months. Flossie, too, would stay all through the school holidays, without ever offering to share the house-keeping expenses. Now all of a sudden she was writing my name on whole chequebooks.

And Gladys was right. Flossie was taken ill in the New Year and Gladys went to the Lynn Road to spend the night – she rushed home at about five in the morning to fetch me, but by the time we got back it was too late and Flossie was gone, just a couple of days before Gladys's birthday. That was a terrible time for Gladys, clearing out the whole house where her mother and Flossie had lived – it took months. Being fifteen years older than Gladys, Flossie had always been like a mother to her as well as a sister, and she was the more dominant personality of the two. Gladys, on the other hand, was shy even with me, never telling me how unhappy she was. I was always very fond of Flossie and I too missed her, but I still had all the interests outside home I'd had when she was alive and I didn't see how lonely Gladys must have been with Flossie gone. That only came to me later, when I found out for myself what it was like to be lonely.

When the Queen came to see us the next year she asked Gladys how her preaching was going, and Gladys had to tell her she'd given it up because she didn't feel well enough to carry on with it. At this time I was still working with my mate Fred Crisp. When I was working on one old people's home Fred would come round sometimes to give me orders, and he fell for an assistant matron there. His first wife had died, and I think this assistant matron reminded him of her, so he married her and Gladys was matron of honour at the weddding.

Later he said to me, 'Ain't your wife getting bloody thin?'

I hadn't noticed, being with her all the time, but he was right. She'd always been such a smart lady, and now her clothes didn't fit her any more. That Sunday when we went to chapel I saw she had her hat on back to front, something Gladys would never do normally. I started to notice how she kept forgetting things – simple things. Then she'd get in a panic about it and hop on her bike before she forgot again what she wanted. She'd cycle down Kent Road to the Gayton Road, the main road, and go straight across it – I saw her do it, she didn't even put her arm out – right into the traffic. She would have been killed over and over again if it hadn't been for the local bus people knowing her, and realising something had gone wrong with her. It came on her so quickly that once I noticed it everyone noticed there was something wrong.

We went to Cambridge, to Addenbrookes Hospital. Gladys was put on a big square bed for tests, with two nurses holding her and moving her whole body up and down. They said they couldn't do anything for her. I got her to go to the home for old people down at South Wootton for the daytime, so that she could be looked after and I could work. A little bus came every day and picked her up in the morning, but she hated it. A telephone call would come to where I was working saying that Gladys had gone missing. The first time no one knew where to look and we were frantic, but the police went out searching. She'd walked two miles from South Wootton to Lynn and gone straight to her father's barber's shop, where she was born. The police found her there drying towels, doing what she used to do for her father when she was a little girl.

We knew where to look after that, but it was no good, I couldn't go on worrying about her like that, and she hated the home. The doctor wanted to put her in another home, and if it hadn't been for the police I was working with, who knew the conditions in that home, she would have gone there. 'For God's sake, Len, don't let Gladys go in that home,' one of them said to me. So for three years I nursed her.

She couldn't hold her water and I had to pack her up like a baby. She was always so ladylike, and now she did everything she would never have done before. Gladys had always come to the Guild Hall with me for the pigeon show, and we took the same seats as we always had. But at half time I had to take her right down the yard where there was an old closet, all in the dark, with an old-fashioned seat made out of wood and nailed above the bowl. There wasn't room for one person, let alone two, and there I was fiddling around packing her up and bringing her back again.

It got much worse. I went to my pigeon friends in Barnsley and Gladys came too, because she'd always liked them. I took her upstairs to bed and she got hold of the runner that was on the dressing table in our room and pulled all the glass bottles and knick-knacks off with it. I think she would have destroyed the room because I just couldn't get through to her, but my friends came and took her downstairs again. They made me go to bed while they sat up with Gladys all night. She wouldn't sleep. We came home the next day.

I think Gladys knew what was happening to her. She'd watched her own mother die of the same thing, and her aunt. I remember when her mother was bad Gladys would say to me, 'Poor thing, it's such a shame to see her like that. She knows, Len, I'm sure she knows what's happening.' And when Gladys herself was bad she would sit in the back room with her face in her hands, just shaking her head and repeating over and over the same sounds, something like 'I di I. I di I,' over and over. God knows what they meant. 'I di-e?' Did she want to die?

The only time I got cross with her was once when she said to me out of the blue, 'I want my mother.' That got to me. The rest of it I could bear, because at least I had her. She was with me. Even when she got to be completely incontinent, poor Gladys, like a poor old cow. In wintertime I would boil up kettles, trying to clean her up. I'd clean her up perfectly, then she'd be back again the next moment in the same state. The very worst was taking her to Yarmouth for a big East Anglia Federation dinner, where I was collecting some prizes. Gladys came up to me and told me she needed to go to the toilet, but we only made it inside the door. There was a woman there, and I don't know who she was but she was an angel. It was all up the walls, all over the floor, exactly like a cow would leave a lady's toilet, and the woman said I wasn't to trouble myself about the mess, she would see to it, I was to look after my wife. Poor Gladys – but I wish she was doing it now rather than not have her.

I knew she was going to die, but I didn't think anything about it until the very second it happened. I suppose it was unthinkable to me. It was a big jolt, that last second, the last breath, to know that Gladys had left me. Senile decay of the brain, the doctor wrote on the certificate. I couldn't shed a tear, not then, not at the funeral. I've missed her every day of my life since.

The routine of caring for pigeons was the only part of my life that was not changed in all that time. Everything else I gave up, but not the birds. While she was ill I had added two pairs of French Dordius stock birds to the lofts. They were very much the same type as the original Belgian stock I'd brought from West Newton because I didn't want to disturb the 'levelness' of my team – that is, their family resemblance. When I say all good flyers breed to a type, it isn't just what they fancy that's bred into their birds, which makes them look all so alike in themselves and different from everyone else's. If he's good the flyer is also responding to what his birds tell him is best in them, and best suited to the particular loft they're living in, the climate outside and within it, its communal spirit, the demands of training, and the road in which the birds compete. Mr Jones, for instance, only raced his cock birds. He didn't fly the widowhood system, which was hardly done at all those days here, so the cocks all lived naturally with their hens in the lofts. But he would have bred for cocks that raced home best to plump, domestic hens. Mr Steele on the other hand, when he took over the Royal Lofts at West Newton, started racing the hens as well as the cocks, breeding for both sexes to race home to each other. Each loft is unique, as is the family of birds within it, and the fancier. The harmony a fancier aims for in his loft is a subtle blending of a thousand circumstances. Who can say how much the Royal Lofts changed once Gladys was no longer there to tend the birds whenever I couldn't?

When I'm gone my birds will move on to become someone else's stock birds. They'll be looked after much as they've always been – there's no such thing as a negligent pigeon man. There's cruelty in the sport – men send their birds to race when they're not fit, or when they're not fully rested from another long race – or perhaps I should say a lacking of pigeon sense. To be accused of lacking in pigeon sense is the worst insult a flyer can conceive of. And I'm not sure I hold with some of the widowhood practices that go on, like using a poor bird's hormones to make him race faster. Bad weather, like cloud, mist or rain, plays havoc with widowhood cocks more than birds racing on the natural system, because of the terrible drive the birds have to get home. They're reckless rather than clever about it.

But the sport demands so much of a man that he has to be committed to it. Just to make a start in it he has to have fallen for the birds in a big way. That's what fanciers have in common, a love for the birds, and each fancier is setting himself up as a trainer of some of the finest athletes in the world, which is a commitment – it's a sport that brings out the best in the men as well as the birds. Every day you have the routine of going to the lofts in the morning with the hope in your heart that all the birds are fit and happy, that no cat has got his paw through the bars during the night and swiped off a bird's head, and that a good recovery is being made by the old birds from the last long race because you want them to win for you next time if they didn't before. Birds thrive on a routine, and they don't have holidays, but there's nothing monotonous about it – every day the birds tell you they're glad to be alive, and it rubs off on you whatever other sorrows your life brings you.

16

Once a Pigeon Man

Before Gladys went, when I came in from the lofts in the mornings I would without fail hear a tapping as I opened the back door. Gladys would be just up and the first thing she always did on coming down the stairs was to tap the glass of the barometer. As I opened the door, tap-tap-tap. I could have told her what it was like outside and whether there was rain in the air, but she couldn't tap me like she did the barometer. You see the little things your other half does every day – the sort of things you never see in yourself because they're too ingrained. Gladys would sit at the table in the breakfast room without turning the chair around, so the chair back was against the wall still and she was sitting sideways.

'Can't you turn that chair around?' I'd say to her.

No answer. She would look at me and she could see right through me, but she never wasted her breath in giving me a list of the irritating ways I had.

People were very kind when I lost Gladys. I had letters of condolence from all over the place, including a lovely one from the Queen, and one from Lady Fermoy. All through that time I would say 'Good morning' most days to Lady Fermoy's son-in-law, Earl Spencer, and he stopped me to say how sorry he was to hear about Gladys's death. He and his family lived on the royal estate at Park House, and both he and Lady Fermoy were close friends of the royal family. Earl Spencer had just split up from his wife, and he would be taking the children, three girls and a boy, to school. It was a private place just up the hill from us on the Gayton Road where they went until they were old enough for the big public schools. I remember clearly Princess Diana as a little girl – she was so pretty and she would say 'Good morning' like her father did. It was a blessing to see the faces of such beautiful children when I was feeling so low.

Clearing out Gladys's things made me realise what she had gone through when Flossie died, and how devastated she must have been, although she'd never told me. When it came to it, I had to be hard with myself and make a proper job of it, but what I couldn't bear to throw out was an old pair of shoes she had always kept in the oven beside the breakfast room fire. When we were first married Gladys had cooked on the fire in the breakfast room. It had a hob and an oven in cast iron built into it, and it worked very well, just like the one my mother had all her life. Gladys would black the stove so it looked good, and with a whistle on the kettle so you knew it had boiled there was no problem with cooking except that it took longer. Gladys was a very good cook, like her mother, but not a plain cook like *my* mother. Gladys did all the fancy dishes, which I understand is a completely different way of doing things, with a lot more washing up at the end of it. Gladys did all that. We kept a fantastic table and I know we ate far too much.

But I remember how Gladys would open a magazine and there would be a lady in high heels standing next to a shining white gas cooker with a thermostat in it, and the advertisement would say how easy to clean it was and explain how you could adjust the flame. Poor Gladys suffered from chilblains like nearly everyone did then and she wanted to make toast without her chilblains playing up – she wanted that gas cooker.

When we got married I'd saved £600 in the Lynn Building Society, and I'd spent £597 of it on the house. Gladys had paid for our honeymoon. I didn't stop saving once we were married, because we'd only managed to furnish a couple of rooms to live in and sleep in, so there was furniture still to buy, and I never bought anything on the never-never – except a New World gas cooker. Gladys and I went down to the showroom and signed up for one, £18 in instalments. I think I made two payments and then I thought I wouldn't have any more of that and I paid it off, which left me with nothing again because I'd been out of work. But Gladys had her cooker, and she was happy; after that she always kept her comfortable shoes in the oven, and that's where they are today.

Gladys wasn't like me. If I'd been ruled by her I'd never have had any money. She loved clothes and she'd never known what it was like to be poor. She'd never learnt any priorities about money like I had from my father. There was the time when he said they couldn't afford a scout's uniform for me – it wasn't that he didn't have the money, because not long after that he bought up half of East Winch. But what he couldn't afford was both, and he was very shrewd. I suppose I get it from him. I don't drink, I don't smoke, and I've never had a car because cars keep you poor. All I've done all my life is save. People up north, like my pigeon friends in North Seaton, they don't have any money but they enjoy life. They would never dream of sacrificing like I have. I thank God I had Gladys so that I enjoyed my life as well, but I can't help being glad that I was my own man with the money I earned. I never kept her short and she had a free hand in what she did with what I gave her, but then she was good at managing. Gladys's Aunt Jenny always used to say about money, 'It's round and it's meant to go round,' and that was how Gladys was, so free and easy and placid – everything I'm not, and I don't know what I did to deserve her.

When the Queen came to see her birds in the New Year, she brought me a Christmas present. That was the only time she did, and it was a lovely thought. I opened this little box by the dining room table, with Her Majesty standing beside me, and I brought out a pair of silver cufflinks. Anyone can tell just by looking at me that I don't wear shirts that take cufflinks, but I was so touched.

'Thank you, Your Majesty,' I said, with a lump in my throat, 'I'll always treasure them.'

The Queen smiled at me, that wonderful smile. 'Make sure you wear them, Mr Rush,' she said, and she dug me gently in the ribs with her finger.

I had to laugh, for she meant so well, and some of the sadness went out of the house. I thought of all the times that Gladys had been with me when the Queen came, and how much Gladys loved her visits. The Queen had come to see us just a week before Prince Edward was born, and Gladys had been amazed at how beautiful she was. 'How glowing with health she is, Len,' Gladys had said when we were alone again. 'I've never seen anyone so beautiful.' Knowing the Queen had brought Gladys a lot of happiness, and I wanted to tell the Queen that, only I couldn't find the right words. So we went down to the lofts instead.

Prince Philip was very sympathetic when I saw him at the Sandringham party that year; he came straight up and said how sorry he was. I remember I wrote a letter of condolence to him one time when his aunt died. He had been at sea on the royal yacht, but the reply he sent me, which was a very nice letter, reached me in less than a day and I always wondered how that had been possible.

Later that year the Queen was in Australia, and so was the England cricket team, playing a Test series against the Australians. Somehow or other the captain of the Australian team, Bill Lawrey, got word to Her Majesty that he was a pigeon man, and knowing she was a pigeon woman he was sure she would allow him, when he came to England later that year, to visit her lofts. It was his heart's desire, he said, to see the royal birds and talk pigeons with the Royal Lofts manager. The Queen said she would be delighted for Lawrey to visit her lofts, and I received word to expect him.

When he came up to Lynn and I saw him sitting on my settee I thought he's only a strip of a fellow – however can he stand up to fast bowlers like Freddie Truman? He made mincemeat of them – they couldn't get Lawrey out no matter how hard they tried. Then we visited the lofts, and he was thrilled with the birds. I showed him one old couple I'd mated together for eight years running and we looked at the young birds they'd just bred – dark beauties they were. The second batch of eggs had already been hatched by foster parents, so I showed him the bloated-looking squabs with a stubble of feathers coming through, always reaching out of the nest for more food.

'I've had more than thirty chicks off this couple and just about half of them have won races,' I told him, 'so I keep breeding from them. Every year the Queen asks what their new young birds have won, because they always win the young bird races. I have arguments with myself about breeding the cock with a young hen, to try for birds that'll win the old bird races more. The cock won for me twice from Thurso, the second time when he was six years old. But I tried putting him with another hen once and he just would not settle – he nearly pecked her head off. You can see he's a gentleman with this hen, proper loving, so I've settled for having a good supply of young bird winners from him. Anyway, the young birds have been good for breeding long-distance birds, so perhaps the cock would always miss a generation with his own young.'

'You know, Len,' Bill Lawrey said, 'in Australia a fancier counts himself lucky if he's got two couples left in the loft at the end of the old bird season. If the cock hasn't got himself eaten by a hawk, the hen will have been brought down by a thunderstorm in the Blue Mountains. Australia is a tough country all right. The birds are decimated regular as clockwork, so we keep breeding from new matings year in year out. I didn't know you could get this kind of consistency in a loft.

The birds are so tame it's amazing.' He gave me back the cock bird we'd been talking about, which he'd been holding for ages.

'This bird's amazing, I'll grant you that,' I said, and I gave it a kiss.

Bill Lawrey laughed at that.

'I always do that,' I told him. 'I had a poultry doctor, one of the powers that be in the poultry world from Norwich, come to see my birds to find out why they're so contented. He did tests on a dozen or sixteen of them, looking – I presume – for a scientific explanation for them being happy. I told him, "This is why they're happy, old mate," and I gave one of the birds a kiss. Of course, the poultry doctor didn't think it was funny at all.'

I took Bill Lawrey around Lynn after we'd had lunch at a pub, and told him how the town had changed so since I was a boy – and since then it has changed as much again. I took him to North End to see the fishing boats. It used to be a colony on its own, with a language of its own, but the fishermen come in their cars now and don't live there in the cottages – the cottages aren't there, either. The fishermen used to have salt in their blood because they were born beside the water and lived all their lives with the boats beyond their doorsteps. All the way from North End men would push hand barrows piled with boxes of cockles and prawns to catch the afternoon train from Lynn Station. I remember them laughing at each other as they ran because it wasn't just the train they were wanting to catch, they wanted to beat each other to it – just to show off.

Savage's is gone from the North End. That was a wonderful business let slip through bad management. It could still be the best joinery firm in the area – it had road, rail and water connections, all three coming right up to it, and some of the best craftsmen in East Anglia. They used to make the fairground roundabouts for the Mart people – the horses and all the woodwork. There's one old carpenter who can do repairs now when the Mart comes to town of a February, and he's good, but what happens when he retires?

I remember how crowded the roads used to be with men like myself pushing hand barrows over cobbled streets at the sort of pace that let you observe the world around you as you went. When I first started going with Gladys, one of her jobs was to take orders from the man who drove the carrier's cart from all the villages round about, every Tuesday, Thursday and Saturday. He would take all the parcels back to the villages and the posh houses in the area. Gladys would take orders for fish and game from the big houses which the man had brought for her, then pass the orders out to the shop. The errand boy would be sent with a hand barrow to where the carrier's cart was pulled up in the yard of a pub, where the big stables were. The roads to the villages were gravel then, so the cart would throw up clouds of dust as it went. And when the wind blew there were showers of dust.

Come October there would be an invasion from the countryside when thousands and thousands of sheep would be driven through the huge archway down the London Road one Tuesday morning to the sheep market. That's where the bus station is now, acres of tarmac, not a whiff of a sheep any more. I think that's when Lynn lost its character, when it lost the sheep market to the bus station and Sainsbury's. When Goddard's the outfitters move, which they will do soon to where the Bird in Hand is being demolished in Norfolk Street, there won't be a single King's Lynn person that owns a shop in the High Street – they'll every one of them be chain stores of one sort or another. And it's not as if the big stores own the land they stand on, so that they become the new proprietors whom the old have to make way for in the nature of things. Even Sainsbury's doesn't own the land beneath it – property developers do.

The shop I miss most in the High Street is Speed the jewellers, which has only recently gone from there. Gladys and I bought our silver service from Speed over the years we were courting and just after we were married – a teapot one year, a sugar bowl the next, then the jug – until we had the whole set, all in solid silver. The son of the Speed we bought it from has grown old and he's had to pack in the shop. It was the son who came and valued the silver after Gladys died, for insurance purposes, and it was a good thing he did because not long after that the whole lot was stolen.

I've had a lot of things stolen over recent years. I wrote and told the Queen about my bike, because I used it to take pigeons to Castle Rising and down to the club in the yard of the Swan. I got a letter back from Major Fellowes saying he understood from the Queen that my bike had been stolen and I was to send an account in to him when I bought a new one. A friend of mine who's a parson found me a lovely old butcher's boy's bike, and the next day I had a cheque from Sandringham. I still use that bike. The birds' baskets fit just right in the front over the small wheel.

Sandringham doesn't change. Of course, Mr Beeching got the royal station at Wolferton, so now the Queen comes to Lynn by train and a car picks her up at the station. The police are everywhere, shutting down the one-way system until the Queen is safely out of it on her way to Sandringham. But if anything Sandringham is even tidier now than it used to be. All the undergrowth is cut from under the trees around the walls of the estate. I like to see some cover for the birds, some undergrowth, but I expect it got in the way of the hunt. Queen Alexandra got rid of the ivy that used to grow in a thick tumble all over the walls, and none has been allowed a foothold since. There's only the ghost of it now, a ghost of a green stain on the red stone walls.

At the last Sandringham party I went to before I retired a gentleman came up to me. The party was in the big ballroom, not the long library, and it was full of people.

'Good evening, Mr Rush,' he said.

'Good evening, sir,' I said. 'Should I know you?'

'Of course,' he said. 'I'm the Keeper of the Privy Purse. I used to come to your house when your wife was alive. I was sorry to hear that she passed away.'

I thanked him.

'I suppose you know all the people here?' he said, and when I told him that I didn't, he went on, 'Now then, don't go away, keep with me. Is there anyone here you would like to meet?'

There was a tall girl with fair hair sitting very close to me in a backless dress, with her back to me. I thought, is that Lady Diana? So I said, 'I'd like to meet that lady there.'

'Madam!' the gentleman called out, although the lady was talking with someone else.

She turned around, and it was the Princess.

'I'd like you to meet this gentleman,' said the Keeper of the Privy Purse. 'This is Len Rush.'

'Not the keeper of Her Majesty's pigeons?' said the Princess.

She had heard of me! We shook hands and I told her, 'I knew you as a little girl, when you went to school at the big house on the hill.'

She laughed. Princess Diana is today what the Queen Mother was to her generation when she was the Duchess of York and then Queen Elizabeth – the beauty of her age, perfect to behold.

'I used to know your grandfather very well indeed,' I told her, 'from when he was President of the King's Lynn Football Club and Norfolk County.'

Her eyes lit up. 'Mr Rush,' she said, 'you must please tell me all you can about my grandfather, because I never saw him. I wasn't born when he died.'

I told her everything I knew – how I remembered him from when I was playing for the town and he would come to the Walks ground for a match and talk to the players, how much it mattered to all of us that he was so interested in the club, and how nice he was. I told her how he died at the Gaywood nursing home while I was blacking out the windows in the war. 'But really I knew your grandmother even better,' I went on, 'because of seeing her every day when she came to visit Lord Fermoy up at Gaywood Hall. She was so worried, but she would always find it in herself to speak with me and be courteous.'

'That sounds like my grandmother,' said the Princess. She gave me the most breathtaking smile. 'I know what you ought to have done, Mr Rush,' she said. 'You ought to have married my grandmother.'

There's only one thing I regret, that I didn't know she was going to say it. Because I would have said, 'Well, the chance would have been a good thing.' But all I could do was think, fancy a Princess saying that to me! Then other people at the party came between us, like they will.

She was so natural, all that sparkling beauty and inside a girl as natural and supple as a fresh stem of willow. I have a tree planter friend who knew Prince Charles from having planted trees on the estate at Sandringham. When he married Diana, Charles asked my friend to go to their house in Gloucestershire to help with planting trees there, and Diana said that he was to bring his family to stay as well. My friend and his wife and child stayed in the house in Gloucestershire like guests, treated just like friends.

It must be so hard for the Princess being in the limelight all her life now, with the security men all around her and just beyond them the press. Just imagine those journalists prying and the photographers killing each other for a shot of the Princess. It must be a terrible strain living like that, but she's so nice and so charming.

I was very glad I was still Royal Lofts manager when I met the Princess. I didn't want to retire, but I couldn't go on for ever. Major Fellowes had retired – everyone has to retire in the end – and I couldn't fool myself I wasn't growing old. Now I'm retired, I still go to the parties at Sandringham, which are held every other year now, but I would not have enjoyed meeting the Princess so much if I'd been the man who used to care for Her Majesty's racing pigeons. I still miss it. The postman never passed my door when I was Royal Lofts manager, but he does now.

The last time the Queen came to my house before I retired she stopped as she was leaving and turned to me, 'You must have a great many friends, Mr Rush,' she said.

'Excuse me, Your Majesty, I haven't,' I said. 'I haven't as many as on the fingers of this hand. I've got no end of acquaintances.'

The Queen was standing in the open doorway, looking at me, and I asked her if she would allow me to read her Gladys's definition of a friend.

The Queen smiled and said yes, so we came back indoors and I went and got my Bible. It's full of markers that Gladys put there, with verses and sayings on them. I found what I wanted and I read it to Her Majesty.

'A friend is a person who knows all about you but loves you just the same, because there's not many people who've not got a skeleton in the cupboard.'

The Queen liked that, and we said goodbye.

The next time I saw her was only to say goodbye again. I was retiring, and to make it official I had to see the Queen in person. After I'd been to church one Sunday the car came from Sandringham to collect me. The Queen was alone in a big room and I was shown in with a dog handler who was changing his job, going to work with horses, I believe. I was being allowed to keep a great many of the Royal birds to race again under my own name, and I thanked the Queen for them. I would have hated more than anything to lose the birds I had bred and loved so, but the new manager, Alan Pearce from Fakenham, only needed a few stock birds for his lofts as I had when the lofts were moved from West Newton to the end of my garden. So I kept on racing the rest, paying my own fee to enter each race and keeping the cash prizes when I won. I don't win so much now. Younger men win, not me. But I wasn't thinking about winning or losing when I said goodbye to the Queen again and handed over care of her birds to another man.

One of my fondest memories is being at the garden party at Buckingham Palace for the Queen Mother's eightieth birthday, and I cling to the memory of her as she was that day, to tell myself it's possible to feel young although I'm old, just as she stays young in herself despite her age. All the people from Sandringham who were invited to the party went up in a coach together. It was a grand affair, because she's such a grand lady, and she found time to talk with me while I was there at the party. I'd met her dozens of times over the years, at Sandringham parties and the flower show in the summer, and it felt like she remembered all those occasions just like I did, as though we were old friends

The Queen Mother's detective, Tony George, became a great friend of mine. He rang me up once, shortly after the Queen had been to see me at Highbury. 'I heard the Queen taking your name in vain, Len,' he said. He'd driven back to London with the Queen Mother and the Queen and he'd heard them talking about me in the car. 'The Queen was saying how much she enjoyed herself at your house, and the Queen Mother was talking about you – your ears must have been ringing.'

He wouldn't say any more, but I was pleased. Anyone would have been.

Many things have changed during my lifetime, not all of them for the better. When my mother died I was heartbroken, helpless like a child again, although I was old enough to expect her to die. But I'd had Gladys with me then, and the minister was always round our house, caring for my mother before she went and for the rest of us who would miss her so. I remember the day she died: the minister came round three times, comforting all of us. I don't expect comfort any more, from the chapel or from anywhere else.

My greatest passion in life from when I was a small boy has always been football, but it sickens me now to see how the footballers go on. I don't like the way they play. I liked the old five forwards, three halfbacks and wingers – and there's none today can compare with the great players from the fifties like Stanley Matthews, Tom Finney, Billy Meredith, Hapgood and Blenkinsop. You can keep your Kevin Keegan and my namesake, Ian Rush. Georgie Best was the Stanley Matthews of his age – he was brilliant, but he was such a damn fool letting women and fame ruin him. He was a child of his time, and the modern world did for him. I'm glad I'm old, because I was born into another world where football was the best and most exciting game men could play. I've been made President of the Lynn club and a life member of the FA, and nothing can take away the pleasure of receiving honours such as that. But I'm more glad than I can say that in all those years pigeon men haven't really changed and the sport of pigeon racing hasn't changed. The love of the birds for the men who care for them can be counted upon, and the men who care for them will always return it.

A NOTE ON THE TYPE

Bembo, the typeface used in this book, is a recutting of a type used by the
scholar-printer Aldus Manutius.

In 1495 Aldus set up a press in Venice, a city which had for some time been
an important printing centre. In the same year he published a tract by Pietro
Bembo in which the type now known as Bembo first appeared.

Bembo (1470–1547), in spite of having a finger cut off in a quarrel as a
youth and being described as having 'fed on amorous and social
opportunities', rose to become a Cardinal as well as one of the most eloquent
spokesmen of the Venetian literary world of the early sixteenth century.

The type, inspired by the calligraphic style of the handwritten manuscripts
of the day, and with capitals which have the characteristics of inscriptional
letters cut in stone, was extremely influential, being the origin of a style of
type design known as 'Old Face' – a style that spread throughout Europe
in the sixteenth century, and remains one of the most frequently used type
styles to this day.

The work of Aldus's press made Venice a major source for the dissemination
of Greek literature throughout the West and thus made a significant
contribution to the Renaissance.